ORRIBLE BRITISH TRUE CRIME

VOLUME ONE

Ben Oakley

Look for more in the Orrible British True Crime Series!

OUT NOW!

Orrible British True Crime Volume 1

From the 17th Century to the 21st, a bonanza collection of 15 short British true crime stories, covering murder, mysteries, mutiny, serial killers, and a mysterious London spanker!

1. The Tom Tackle Pub Murder

A young woman was brutally attacked and murdered outside a popular Southampton pub, resulting in a 30-year-long miscarriage of justice and the creation of Operation Iceberg.

2. Monster of Cannock Chase

Raymond Morris, known as the A34 Killer, Babes in the Ditch murderer, or Monster of Cannock Chase, killed three girls and abused many more, leading to one of the largest manhunts in British history.

3. Hammersmith Nude Murders

If Jack the Ripper has gripped imaginations for over 100 years, then the story of Jack the Stripper in 1960s London, is enough to send chills to the darkest parts of your soul.

4. Tome Raiders: The Great British Book Heist

From a London customs warehouse to an underground room in Romania, here's how thieves stole £2.5million worth of books and how detectives tracked them down.

5. Bow Cinema Axeman

During the Golden Age of movies, a cinema attendant took an axe to his manager and eloped with a suitcase full of money, in a tale of premeditated murder, historical horrors, and a fake death.

6. The Freddy Krueger Killer

A man inspired by horror movies went on a rampage that left four dead and two injured, in a tragic case that laid the blame at the feet of those put in place to protect the public.

7. The Tale of The Man They Could Not Hang

An Englishman sentenced to death was led up the steps of the gallows to be executed, but despite multiple attempts, he dodged the noose, leading to a strange tale of murder and luck.

8. Nude in the Nettles

A strange phone call leads to the discovery of a woman's body on the North York Moors, but for over 40 years, her identity and death remain a mystery, and one of England's oddest unsolved cold cases.

9. The World's End Murderer

Angus Sinclair was a dangerous predator capable of sinking to the depths of depravity, convicted of four murders and linked to many more, he was one of Britain's worst serial killers.

10. Great Coram Street Murder

In Victorian London, a lady of the night was found in her room with her throat slashed, and the door locked from the outside. Read the story of one of the oldest unsolved murders in London.

11. The Horrors of Dennis Nilsen

The sickening tale of British serial killer Dennis Nilsen, who killed 15 young men, and dissected some of their remains – before flushing them down the toilet and blocking the sewers with flesh.

12. The Mary Russell Murders

In 1828, the Mary Russell brig floated into Cork Harbour, with seven of its crew dead. They had been brutally murdered by their Captain, and the survivors had a disturbing story to tell.

13. The Reality TV Swindler

How a down-on-his-luck homeless man conned fame-seeking wannabes to take part in a year-long reality TV show that didn't exist.

14. Murder at Beachy Head

A young woman disappeared near Beachy Head, a known suicide spot, but nine years later, her body is discovered on top of the cliffs, with links to an infamous serial killer.

15. The Cracks Terror

In old London, women were arming themselves and men were crossdressing to catch a mysterious buttock beater, who would lift women's skirts and spank them before retreating to the dark alleyways.

The Tom Tackle Pub Murder

A young woman was brutally attacked and murdered outside a popular Southampton pub, resulting in a 30-year-long miscarriage of justice and the creation of Operation Iceberg.

Southampton on the South Coast of England is famous for its cruise ship harbour, shopping centres, many Universities, and the last port of call for the Mayflower ship that transported English Pilgrims to the New World of America in 1620.

It's also known for murder but you won't find placards about that in the city's museum. One particularly infamous murder took place in 1979, when 22-year-old Teresa Elena De Simone was raped and strangled to death as she got into her car outside the Tom Tackle pub.

What makes this murder so infamous and interesting is that the person ultimately convicted of her murder was innocent and was incarcerated for 27 years before an appeal proved he had not killed her. Instead, it turned out that Teresa had been attacked and killed by a baby-faced 17-year-old boy named David Lace.

Even when he confessed to police he was the murderer, they refused to believe him, and let an innocent man rot in jail for 27 years. Lace's parents were so moved by the murder, they placed an obituary in the local paper that said, '*God only knows why*,' not knowing it was their son who was the culprit.

Fateful night

Teresa was born in 1957 to Mary and Mario de Simone of Italian heritage. When her parents split, her mother married Michael Sedotti and they moved to the residential Shirley area of Southampton, where Teresa grew up in a happy household.

She was known to be a shy but popular girl at school and graduated with good grades that enabled her to get a job as a clerk for the Southern Gas Board, now the British Gas building in the centre of the city, where she worked until her death.

Southampton is also known for its many bars and nightclubs, propped up by the student population that threads through the city. Like any young woman, Teresa had a good social life and was often out drinking in the city on Friday and Saturday nights.

To increase her savings, she took a second part-time evening job at the Tom Tackle pub which was located next to the Mayflower Theatre at the time. Taking the pub job meant that she could broaden her social circle further.

On 4th December 1979, Teresa finished her evening shift at the pub and left with her friend Jenni Savage to go to a local nightclub in the nearby student area of London Road, to celebrate another friend's birthday.

Despite London Road being within walking distance, Jenni decided to drive them both there, and would drop Teresa off to the Tom Tackle car park to collect her own car later on. When they arrived at the club at around 11pm, they had some drinks with friends but decided to leave an hour later.

Jenni drove them back to the Tom Tackle car park where they stayed in the car chatting for about half an hour. Teresa then left to get into her own car. Jenni watched Teresa in the rear-view mirror to see if she got into her car safely, then drove home. It was the last time Teresa was seen alive.

Body in the back seat

The location of the pub in Commercial Road was only 100 metres from the main Southampton police station and courts of law, which enraged locals when the murder wasn't solved straight away. The following morning, Teresa's mother discovered she had not come home and became concerned.

She and Teresa's stepfather drove to the pub to find Teresa's car still parked up. Believing her to have stayed the night elsewhere, they thought nothing else of it. An hour later, landlord of the Tom Tackle, Anthony Pocock, was expecting a delivery but Teresa's car was blocking the cellar door.

When he went to try and move it himself, he recoiled with horror when he saw Teresa's partially nude body on the back seat. The police arrived within minutes and cornered off the pub, as it was now the scene of a murder.

Teresa was naked from the waist down with her breasts exposed. Her underwear was around her ankles and she had been strangled to death after being raped. A pathologist put the time of death at between 1am and 2am, just a few minutes after Jenni had driven away.

It was suspected that the culprit was either hiding in the shadows watching the two girls, or was waiting in Teresa's car, and made his move when Jenni drove off. The cause of death was strangulation but the pathologist confirmed that due to the white frothy mucous in her mouth, it had been a slow and painful strangulation.

The gold crucifix she was wearing had been taken from her and may have been used as a ligature. It led the local press to label the culprit as the Crucifix Killer, but that moniker didn't last long. Incidentally, the cross was never found.

Despite the murder taking place in the days before DNA profiling, police took swabs, fingerprints and other forensic data which was stored for decades, despite officials claiming it had been destroyed a few years after. The forensic evidence led to the discovery of the real killer 30 years later.

It became one of the largest investigations in Southampton police history. No immediate arrest was made, and in the year that followed, they interviewed approximately 30,000 people, took 2,500 statements and tracked 500 people who had been in the area on the night of the murder. None of which pointed them towards a suspect.

The innocent man

As early as two days after the murder, a man named Sean Hodgson was arrested for stealing from a parked car. He had arrived in Southampton from County Durham two days earlier – the night of the murder. Was it coincidence or something more sinister?

The theft from a vehicle and having arrived in Southampton the night of the murder certainly seemed to point to Hodgson as a suspect. But despite the coincidences, Hodgson's blood type was O and the killer's was A.

Other factors seemed to point away from Hodgson when police received letters from an unidentified writer claiming to know the location and identity of the killer. There were also two anonymous phone calls to Southampton police from a young man claiming to be the killer but they were not taken seriously.

On 16th May 1980, Hodgson pleaded guilty to theft from a vehicle and was granted bail awaiting sentencing. When he was arrested in London on a similar offence a month later, he was sentenced to three years in prison, where he confessed to multiple crimes as a way of bolstering his image in prison, many of which were untrue.

A year after the murder, almost to the day, Hodgson confessed to a priest that he had killed a woman near the Tom Tackle pub in Southampton. Hodgson was escorted from prison to the car park of the Tom Tackle, where it was written he gave details about the case that only the killer could have known.

That Hodgson turned out to be innocent was something of an oddity, he had spent time in a psychiatric hospital before moving to Southampton, and his delusions may have been playing with him. It was also suspected police fed him some of the unreleased details of the murder so that they could finally pin it on someone.

At the same time, he also confessed to two other murders, both of which turned out to be untrue and had never taken place. At the trial, he confessed to being a pathological liar due to his mental condition and confessed to unsolved crimes he didn't commit because he wanted someone to pay for them.

The prosecution posited a story that Hodgson had got drunk, fell asleep in Teresa's car, which was unlocked, and then attacked her when she entered the vehicle. In February 1982, Hodgson was found guilty of murder and sentenced to life in prison.

Something was untoward

He was denied parole multiple times for continuously claiming he was innocent, something that would pose a risk if an offender was released. 26 years later, in 2008, Hodgson contacted London solicitors, Julian Young and Co. who specialised in bringing appeals against convictions.

The lead solicitor, Rag Chand, spent four months attempting to trace the forensic evidence from the scene of the murder, but was constantly told it had been destroyed in 1998 in accordance with best practices.

Unwilling to give in and going with a gut feeling that something was untoward, Chand was directed to an evidence archive on an industrial estate in the Midlands, which appeared to be unused and unprotected. It was there, he found the forensic evidence he needed.

In early 2009, after DNA analysis of the semen swab, it was confirmed that they did not come from Hodgson, which meant he was not the killer and was innocent. The only crime he had committed was a theft from a vehicle and multiple confessions due to his mental capability.

In February 2009, after 27 years in prison as an innocent man, Hodgson was released to public fanfare – and disgust at the system that had kept him captive for most of his life. Prior to his release, Hodgson had been diagnosed with schizophrenia and depression. He received a paltry £250,000 in compensation.

He received no care after his release and a year later was in court again over allegations of rape and sexual assault of a woman with learning difficulties. He was sentenced to a community order that involved intense psychiatric care.

In 2012, just three years after his release, Hodgson died of emphysema, a smoking-related disease. But two big questions remained; who had killed Teresa and where was he hiding?

Operation Iceberg

A month after Hodgson had been released, and armed with forensic evidence, police reopened the Teresa murder case and called it Operation Iceberg, assumed to be because of the length of time the case had been truly unsolved, and as cold as a cold case could get.

No matches were found in a search of the DNA database but police pressed on to test as many of the original suspects as possible and spent many months going through old statements and papers relating to the case.

Half a year later, genetic familial testing discovered a possible link to a suspect. A sibling of a man named David Lace was found to have a partial match to the DNA they had on record. Unfortunately for the investigation, Lace had taken his own life in 1988 for reasons then unknown.

In the summer of 2009, Lace's body was exhumed in a cemetery in neighbouring city Portsmouth and it was confirmed that the forensic evidence matched Lace. It would have been a billion-to-one chance for it to be someone else.

Then police uncovered what they already suspected but feared wasn't true. Lace had already confessed he was the killer to police back in 1983 while in custody on unrelated charges. But because Hodgson had been convicted of the murder, the police ignored it.

It was also suggested but never confirmed that Lace was the person who had phoned the police station and sent the letters in the days following the murder. He had been arrested in 1980 and charged with theft. When he committed more burglaries while on probation, he was arrested again and sentenced to five years in prison.

Secrets to the grave

Lace was released from Dartmoor prison in 1987, and less than a year later took his own life without an obvious motive. It's clear now that he couldn't cope with the guilt of what he had done and that an innocent man had gone to jail instead of him.

His family claimed he had become depressed since his release, gave away his possessions, apologised to them for his past actions, and resigned from his new job – all signs of suicidal ideation. He was found dead by his landlord on 9th December 1988, just over nine years to the day that he had killed Teresa.

In his statement to police back in 1983, Lace said that he was outside the Tom Tackle pub when Jenni dropped Teresa back to her car. When Teresa got into her car, he knocked on the window then forced his way in, locking the doors behind him.

He described how he raped her and strangled her using the seatbelt of the passenger seat. He then stole her handbag and jewellery to make it look like a robbery. He hid in the shadows for ten minutes before catching a train back to Portsmouth where he lived at the time.

But police didn't believe him because they thought the real killer was already in jail. As a result of the case, new laws were introduced that meant all evidence would remain accessible until a convicted person was released, something which would have led to Hodgson's release many years earlier.

It was a bittersweet ending to a case that had let an innocent man rot in jail for almost 30 years, left a promising young woman dead, and a suicide with dark secrets that were taken to the grave.

Monster of Cannock Chase

Raymond Morris, known as the A34 Killer, Babes in the Ditch murderer, or Monster of Cannock Chase, killed three girls and abused many more, leading to one of the largest manhunts in British history.

Though the Moors Murders are well known in the country today, when Ian Brady and Myra Hindley killed five children between 1963 and 1965, the Cannock Chase murders were as infamous in the latter half of the 1960s.

Factory worker Raymond Leslie Morris killed at least three young girls between 1965 and 1967, virtually picking up where the Moors Murderers had left off. Also known as the A34 Killer, the Babes in the Ditch murderer, or The Monster of Cannock Chase, Morris was the subject of one of the largest manhunts in British history.

The murders took place in and around the nature park of Cannock Chase in Staffordshire, home to sprawling forests and plentiful hiking trails. Cannock Chase also played an important part in the First World War, where two large military training camps were built due to its inland location.

Yet it is more known for the location where the bodies of three young girls between the ages of 5 and 7 were found. Over the years, Morris has been linked to other attempted murders and sexual assaults, making him one of the most prolific child killers in British history.

Uncle Len

The tale of the Cannock Chase Murderer began with a brutal attack on nine-year-old Julie Taylor. As she walked home in the late evening of 2nd December 1964, a car pulled up alongside her, and inside was a man calling himself Uncle Len, claiming to be a friend of Julie's mother.

She was lured into his car on the pretence that they had to go and pick up Christmas presents from Julie's auntie. Julie agreed but became nervous when they drove past her auntie's house, and onwards to the mining village of Bentley where they parked up near an old mining waste ground. It was there that Uncle Len made his true intentions known.

Julie was raped multiple times, abused, tortured, and strangled. She was then thrown from the car into a nearby ditch. As luck would have it, less than an hour later, a passing cyclist heard Julie's whimpers and discovered her half-naked and damaged body.

Had the cyclist not found her, then she most certainly would have died from her wounds, which were extensive. She had suffered major internal injuries and was rushed to the hospital covered in blood and bruises.

Unknown to the area at the time, Raymond Leslie Morris had begun his campaign of abuse and violence and was later linked to Julie's attack. It appeared that Uncle Len was Morris, and Julie was his first known victim.

Murder of the innocents

Almost a year later, in Aston, on 8th September 1965, six-year-old Margaret Reynolds disappeared on her way back to school after lunch. The route she had taken was short and obvious, difficult for someone to lose their way. At some point on the track, she vanished.

Despite a large investigation involving 160 police officers and 25,000 interviews, no trace of her was found. The locals were so invested in the disappearance that every single house was searched within an eight mile radius of the school but to no avail, she had simply disappeared.

In the weeks before Julie's disappearance, police received reports of a single white man driving around and asking young girls to get into his car. Some had been sexually assaulted but managed to get away or were let go by the man after he had penetrated them with his fingers. The man was never found but was later suspected to be Morris.

Five days after Christmas, in the same year, five-year-old Diana Tift vanished as she walked home alone from her grandmother's home in the early afternoon. Diana never made it home and was reported missing almost immediately.

Already disturbed by Margaret's disappearance three months earlier, local residents amassed a 2,000-strong search team to look for her, with various rewards popping up. As they searched for Diana, the realisation dawned that a child abductor was in their midst and had been responsible for both girls disappearances.

Police immediately made the connection to the 1964 attack on Julie Taylor and moved the search towards the Cannock Chase area of natural beauty. An additional 500 officers from the West Midlands region were put on the case to find the missing girls.

They searched gardens, sheds, greenhouses, lakes, rivers, ponds, and wooded areas but there was no sign of Diana or Margaret. Then two weeks later on 12th January 1966, a man hunting rabbits at Mansty Gully on Cannock Chase made a gruesome discovery.

Macabre discovery

The man had stumbled upon the half-naked body of Diana, somewhat hidden in the undergrowth of a drainage ditch, less than half a mile from the main A34 road. As the man raised the alarm he noticed something else further up the ditch but wasn't quite sure what he was looking at.

What appeared to be a mass of leaves and twigs, turned out to be the decomposed nude body of Margaret Reynolds. It appeared the girl's killer had used the same dumping ground to hide his crimes and in the case of Margaret had somewhat succeeded, as due to the decomposition, pathologists were unable to confirm a cause of death.

Diana had been raped and suffocated with her own coat when the killer covered her nose and mouth. Police were forced to put out a press release stating that they were hunting a dangerous child killer who may strike again. And in that degree, they were right, as Morris could not contain his dark desires longer than a few months.

Despite the massive nationwide manhunt for the killer of the two girls, it would be almost two years before Morris was finally caught but in that time he was free to attack many more. At one point police suspected the rabbit hunter to be the killer as he had a violent past but he was ruled out due to early forensic testing.

On 14th August 1966, 10-year-old Jane Taylor was abducted while riding her bike in the Cheshire village or Mobberley, 50 miles away from Cannock Chase. Police linked her disappearance to the murders around Cannock Chase but no trace of her was found at the time and having the same surname as Julie Taylor was only a coincidence.

Another murder

A year-and-a-half after the bodies of Diana and Margaret had been found, the police search and investigation had dwindled due to the lack of information that was coming in. There were fewer avenues to pursue and lesser leads.

They resorted to preparing for the next incident and put a plan in place to have roadblocks set up within 20 minutes of a reported abduction. The plan of waiting for another abduction sent the public into a panic and accusations of shoddy police work were thrown around in the press.

Then, on 19th August 1967, just as the cases were going cold, seven-year-old Christine Darby was abducted as she played with friends in Caldmore,

Walsall, ten miles from Cannock Chase. The driver asked for directions but lured Christine into the car as he feigned being confused about where to go.

Her friends raised the alarm and the police were called almost immediately. The plan of implementing roadblocks was put into place and a circle was drawn around Walsall to prevent the car, considered to be grey by Christine's friends, from getting past them.

The plan failed and suddenly they had another missing young girl on their hands, and an angry public protesting against them. Another large search was put together to find Christine in the hope she may still be alive somewhere.

Her friends insisted the man spoke with a local accent and drove a grey car, backing up initial police belief's that they were dealing with a local man close to Cannock Chase. Three hundred officers and some off-duty soldiers began the arduous task of searching the large nature park.

Three days later on 22nd August, one of the soldiers stumbled across Christine's nude body, barely hidden in the undergrowth of a wooded patch. The body was found less than a mile from the location of Diana and Margaret.

She was found spreadeagled on her back with blood soaked into the ground beneath her. Her tongue protruding from her mouth confirmed she had been suffocated to death. She had been raped and murdered in the very location she had been found.

Massive investigation

As the investigation went into overdrive, police realised they were dealing with a serial killer, with a weakness for young girls. All three of the murdered girls lived within 17 miles of each other, and close to the A34 road, leading to some reporters calling them the A34 Murders.

As police had found the body shortly after death, the area was descended upon by forensic experts and detectives. They found tyre tracks leading in and out of the wooded area, clearly made by the killer due to where the tracks had stopped.

In the week that followed, over 600 vehicles were traced and ultimately ruled out of the investigation. Two hikers in Cannock Chase remembered seeing a grey vehicle parked in the woods and noted a man with dark hair nearby. All reports suggested the vehicle was a grey Austin A55 or A60.

In the months that followed, a special incident room was set up to track 23,000 owners of Austin vehicles in the Midlands, involving 200 officers and a purpose built evidence storage unit. The search expanded to interview 44,000 owners of Austin vehicles outside the Midlands.

Using witness accounts, and for the first time in British history, police created a colour facial composite of the man they suspected was the killer. It ended up being published on the front pages of many national British newspapers.

For the next year, police interviewed several thousand suspects but nothing came of it. They set up an initiative to interview every man in the county but it failed due to the massive scale of the operation. Once again, the killer had escaped capture – until the next abduction was rumbled.

A final abduction

On 4th November 1968, 10-year-old Margaret Aulton was playing near the side of a road throwing wood onto an unlit bonfire in preparation for Guy Fawkes night the next day, when a car pulled up next to her, and the man asked if she would like some free fireworks.

When Aulton refused, the man tried to forcibly drag her into the car but she managed to break free and run away. An 18-year-old named Wendy Lane was exiting a chip shop opposite when she witnessed the attempted abduction and ran towards the car, causing the man to drive off at high speed.

Fortunately, Aulton was not abducted, and more fortunately, Lane managed to note down the number plate, colour, and make of car; a green Ford Corsair. Police were led to 39-year-old Raymond Leslie Morris who lived in a council estate block – directly opposite Walsall police station.

It turned out that police had already interviewed him four times relating to the abductions and murders but his wife had given an alibi each time. On 15th November, Morris was arrested and charged with the murder of Christine Darby. His wife confirmed she had given a false alibi based on what Morris had told her.

To back up the charge, police executed a warrant on Morris's house and found a box full of homemade child pornography, most of whom involved the same girl, later discovered to be his five-year-old niece. He was originally charged with the murder of Christine Darby due to a witness placing him at the scene, the attempted abduction of Margaret Aulton, and a charge of indecent assault against his niece.

He pleaded guilty to abusing his niece but innocent to any connection with the murders and abductions, something he would protest until the end of his days. The trial was built on the basis of two eye-witness statements claiming that Morris was the man they'd seen in the car or near the crime scene.

There was no forensic evidence put forward to prove Morris was the killer. Circumstantial evidence including petrol station receipts, employment clocking-off cards, and timelines when he wasn't with his family, were seemingly enough to convict him on.

On 18th February 1969, Morris was found guilty of the murder of Christine, the attempted abduction of Aulton, and the abuse of his niece, leading to a life sentence. But who was Morris? Why had he killed the girls? And was he truly the culprit?

A violent past

Morris had lived in Walsall all his life and was known to be sexually dominant, violent to his previous partners, and had a high level of intelligence. In 1966, he was arrested while taking photographs of two underage girls who he had lured to his council flat – something the police investigation never connected to the later murders. He was let go due to no evidence found in the flat.

It was clear that Morris had a dark taste for young girls, whom he could control and exert dominance over. That he was never considered a strong suspect was damaging to the police investigation, and many considered his wife should have been charged with providing a false alibi.

Despite never being charged with the murders of Diana Tift and Margaret Reynolds, or the disappearance of Jane Taylor, the cases were closed as Morris fitted the profile, along with the fact that Christine's body was found near the other two girls, despite no evidence suggesting it was Morris.

The families of the dead and missing hold strong beliefs that Morris was the perpetrator, along with the fact that the murders and abductions stopped in the area after his arrest.

But in 2010, after 41 years in prison, Morris was granted a review in a bid to overturn his conviction as there was no forensic evidence to conclude he had killed Christine, only circumstantial and via two witnesses. Incidentally, if the trial had been carried out today, the evidence would not have been enough to convict him of the murder.

The monster

Incidentally, Morris never confessed and maintained his innocence right up until his death of leukaemia in 2014, having spent 45 years in prison. Among his last words were, '*I didn't do it, and I hope that someone will listen.*'

If not Morris then who? The disappearance of 10-year-old Jane Taylor 50 miles away from Cannock Chase ended when her skeletal remains were found in 1972 in North Wales, six years after her disappearance.

She had been murdered by a man named William Ian Copeland, who confessed to another inmate while he was in jail on unrelated charges. Copeland was charged and convicted of her murder in 1975. Like Morris's trial, the conviction was based on circumstantial evidence but in that instance, Copeland confessed.

There are some who suspect that Copeland may have had a hand in the murders of Margaret and Diana, and even Christine but he was already in prison for two of them and was not known to live in the area at the time.

It seems unusual that the cases of Margaret and Diana were never tried in a court of law, and the only assumption one can make is that if they had done then the minimal evidence against Morris would have seen him walk free.

That Morris didn't confess to Christine's murder was perhaps the last bit of control he had left, hoping that one day he would be retried and found innocent, free to rape and kill again. Morris abused many girls including his own niece, had a predilection for child pornography, and even took pictures of underage girls in his flat.

Morris killed three young girls and dumped their bodies in Cannock Chase, their dignity wrecked, ripped away by a monster hiding in plain sight. If he had not been caught then it's likely that the Monster of Cannock Chase would have continued to kill, leaving families destroyed in his wake.

Hammersmith Nude Murders

If Jack the Ripper has gripped imaginations for over 100 years, then the story of Jack the Stripper in 1960s London, is enough to send chills to the darkest parts of your soul.

In comparison to countries like the United States, the United Kingdom has very few serial killers, and even fewer unsolved cases of serial killers. One of the most famous of the unsolved serial murderers is the Jack the Ripper story which has gripped imaginations for over 100 years.

But between 1964 and 1965 in West London, six prostitutes were strangled to death and their nude bodies discarded in or near the River Thames. Despite intense scrutiny in documentaries, books, and new imaginations, the murders have never been solved.

Here we look at the true story behind one of London's – and the UK's – most notorious, yet little spoken about unsolved serial killer cases. The press came to call him Jack the Stripper, and the murders were collectively known as the Hammersmith Nude Murders.

Nude murders

Though there were two prior murders that were later linked to Jack the Stripper, we'll look at the spate of six first.

Victim number one was 30-year old Hannah Tailford, found on the Thames foreshore in Upper Mall, Hammersmith on 2nd February 1964. The Northumberland-born woman was found nude with some of her teeth missing and her underwear stuffed into her mouth. She had been strangled and drowned.

Victim number two was 25-year-old Nottinghamshire-born Irene Lockwood, who was found dead in Duke's Meadow, Chiswick, on 8th April 1964. She had been strangled and drowned and was left nude on the foreshore of the Thames. Lockwood was pregnant at the time.

Victim number three was 22-year-old Scottish born Helen Barthelemy who was strangled to death and left in an alleyway in Brentford on 24th April 1964. A sex worker since the age of 16, she was found partially nude with torn clothing.

Victim number four was 30-year-old Mary Fleming from Scotland. Her nude body was found in Chiswick close to the Thames on 14th July 1964. She had been strangled to death. Nearby residents had heard a car reversing shortly before the body was found.

Victim number five was 21-year-old Frances Brown whose decomposing body was found in a car park in Kensington on 25th November 1964. She had been strangled to death and dumped partially nude. A friend and colleague of Brown claimed she had been missing since October after last being seen getting into a client's grey Ford Zephyr.

The sixth victim in the spate of six, was 27-year-old Bridget O'Hara, whose nude body was discovered on the Heron Trading Estate in Acton, on 16th February 1965. She had been drowned and her body displayed near a small electric substation. Bizarrely, it appeared her body had been kept warm before being dumped.

Figg & Rees

Though the six victims are considered to have been carried out by the same person, there were two prior murders that have since been linked over time. Both bearing remarkably similar traits to the six above.

The first of the additional victims was 21-year-old Elizabeth Figg, she was found in the early hours of the morning by two police officers on their regular route on 17th June 1959.

She was found partially nude on the north bank of the River Thames at Duke's Meadow, Chiswick. It was a familiar location to the officers, as prostitutes used the park as a place to take their clients. Irene Lockwood, the second of the spate victims, was also found in Duke's Meadow.

Elizabeth had been strangled to death. Her body had been found with her dress torn to the waist and ripped open to expose her breasts. Her underwear and shoes were missing and were never found. She was identified after a post-mortem picture distributed to the press was recognised by her mother.

She was also known to have carried a white handbag which was never found. It was suspected in the initial investigation that she had been murdered in a car and then her body disposed of on the shrubland near the Thames.

A local pub landlord, who lived on the other side of the river, claimed he had seen carlights in the area after midnight and may have heard the scream of a woman.

On 29th September 1963, 22-year-old Welsh prostitute Gwynneth Rees was found dead in Mortlake. She was found at the Barnes Borough Council household refuse disposal site, close to the Thames.

She was completely nude aside from a single black stocking hanging off her right foot. Gwynneth suffered an additional dishonour in death when workmen accidentally decapitated her with a shovel when flattening the rubbish.

Going nowhere

By the death of Helen Barthelemy, the third of the six, police were beginning to suspect they had a serial murderer on their hands. Helen's death gave them their first clue, which were flecks of paint used in car manufacturing.

The same type of miniscule flakes were found at the scene of Bridget O'Hara's murder. Police believed the flakes to have come from the killer's workplace and spent a lot of the early days attempting to trace it to local businesses.

By the Spring of 1965, two months after the last murder, the police had interviewed over 7,000 suspects but still had no idea who the perpetrator was. They had managed to match the paint flecks to a concealed transformer, located near to where O'Hara was found.

A paint spraying shop was located on the same industrial estate which meant the flakes could have been lifted up in the middle of the night and placed at some of the crime scenes to throw the investigation off the scent. The paint clues and the constant interviewing had led them nowhere – at least, not yet.

Due to mounting public pressure and intense media scrutiny, the police decided to play a dangerous game with the killer.

The bluff

Chief Superintendent John Du Rose of Scotland Yard was the detective put in charge of the Hammersmith Nude Murders investigations. He and his team had exhausted all avenues and decided to put pressure on the killer through a series of bluffs.

In the Spring, Du Rose held a press conference where and his team announced the police had narrowed down the suspect list to just 20 men. He said that by using an ongoing process of elimination, each suspect was being purged from the investigation until they got down to one.

But Du Rose was calling the killer's bluff. Despite interviewing over 7,000 suspects, they were no closer to catching the killer at all. The investigation decided that at the very least they could put pressure on the killer not to kill again and even force a surrender.

A few days later, Du Rose held another press conference and claimed they had narrowed the suspects down to ten. Another few days passed and another press conference took place where conveniently the suspect list had decreased to just three.

Though the crimes remain unsolved, the Hammersmith Nude Murders stopped and the unidentified killer seemingly vanished into thin air.

Profumo Affair

At the time of the murders, and in the decades that followed, many suspects have been named, with some being more plausible than others.

Shortly after the press conferences, a 57-year-old caretaker named Kenneth Archibald walked into Notting Hill Police Station and confessed to killing Irene Lockwood. He was eventually taken to trial but pleaded not guilty, claiming he had lied about the confession. He was later acquitted but the false confession meant police may have let the real killer get away.

In three books about the killings, *Jack of Jumps* by David Seabrook, *Found Naked and Dead* by Brian McConnell, and *Laid Bare: The Nude Murders and the Hunt for 'Jack the Stripper'* by Dick Kirby, the authors point towards a member of the Metropolitan Police as the suspect.

Seabrook claimed that many senior detectives in the Met believed a former police detective was responsible for the killings. The officer has never been named and many researchers believe the Met covered up the involvement of one of their own, hence why it has never been solved.

Later researchers suggested many of the victims were known to engage in the underground party and sex scene. It was suspected some of the victims had appeared in porn films and were known to have mild connections to something called the Profumo Affair.

The Profumo Affair became a major scandal when John Profumo, the British Secretary of State for War, was revealed to be having an extramarital affair with 19-year-old model Christine Keeler. The investigation into the affair unveiled tales of sex parties and underground porn, ultimately ending the Macmillan Conservative Government in 1963.

The theory was that some of the victims may have had information that could have further damaged the British Government. Thus they were killed off to make it look like a serial killer did it, to silence them and throw the investigation off the scent.

Suspects

Du Rose maintained the killer was a Scottish security guard named Mungo Ireland, who worked on the Heron Trading Estate where the final victim O'Hara was found. He claimed the flecks of paint at some of the crime scenes were because Ireland worked near to where the paint spraying shop was.

When Ireland's name was mentioned as a possible suspect, he took his own life through carbon monoxide poisoning. A later investigation revealed that Ireland had alibis stating he was in Scotland at the time of all the murders.

The former British light-heavyweight boxing champion Freddie Mills was accused of being the killer in research for a book by gangster Jimmy Tippett, Jr. He claimed that many London gangsters knew Mills was the killer.

This was corroborated by a freelance journalist named Peter Neale who told police he had received word that '*Mills did it*'. Despite the suspicion, Mills was found shot dead in his car in the Summer of 1965. Though reported as a suicide, some believe he had been murdered to cover up the truth.

Back in 1921, Welshman Harold Jones had killed two girls from his hometown. On 21st June, he raped and killed 8-year-old Freda Burnell. 17 days later he killed his 11-year-old neighbour Florence Little. Jones was just 15-years-old at the time of both murders.

He was arrested and handed down a life sentence, but released 20 years later in 1941, at the age of 35. In 1947, Jones was known to be living in Fulham, London. Records show that he left Fulham in 1962, and his whereabouts between 1962 to 1965 – the time of the Nude Murders – remains unknown. Jones died in Hammersmith in 1971.

Due to poor police record-keeping at the time, he was never considered a suspect when the initial investigation began. A BBC documentary in 2019 called *Dark Son: The Hunt for a Serial Killer*, concluded there were many similarities between the murders Jones had committed as a boy and the Jack the Stripper murders.

Victims of choice

The murder of a prostitute is especially difficult for police and other law enforcement. The very nature of the victim having had sex with multiple men and the interactions with hundreds, if not thousands of strangers, makes it even harder to investigate.

They are also less likely than most rape or assault victims to report the crimes to police for exactly the same reason.

There was a belief that law enforcement agencies wouldn't even worry too much about prostitutes being murdered and saw them as lower-class citizens. Another reason was that some officers throughout history had used prostitutes themselves and didn't want anything linking back to them.

Record-keeping and crime detection in the 1960s were far more difficult and disorganised than they are in today's digital world. Improvements in evidence collection and statistical data processes are at a far greater level nowadays.

Simply put, in the early to mid-20th Century, it was easier to get away with serial killing than in later decades, partly because victims were easier to find.

Cold case deluxe

Jack the Ripper continues to dominate tours of London, and the Yorkshire Ripper continues to make headline news, even after his death. Why is it that the murder of eight women in West London, the clear work of a serial killer, doesn't reach the headlines as often?

Did the Met cover up the real name of the suspect to protect themselves? Were government officials involved in silencing prostitutes for fear of repercussions? Was Harold Jones unable to relinquish the dark desires of his youth and ultimately get away with eight more murders?

Many records of the case are still on file with the police, including evidence collected from the bodies. Even with advances in DNA technology, new investigators are struggling to connect the dots and to agree on a suspect.

Despite periodic checks by the Metropolitan Police, the case remains cold, and is subject to speculation at every turn. We may never know if the police bluff worked – or simply forced the killer so far underground that there was never any chance of him being caught.

Tome Raiders: The Great British Book Heist

From a London customs warehouse to an underground room in Romania, here's how thieves stole £2.5million worth of books and how detectives tracked them down.

The Frontier Forwarding customs warehouse in Feltham, London, near Heathrow Airport, is generally used to temporarily store valuable items that travel in and out of Britain. On the evening of 29th January 2017, the warehouse was home to many rare books destined for a major trade fair in California.

Like something out of a Hollywood movie, two acrobatic thieves executed a quite remarkable robbery that stands up as one of Britain's most daring and unusual of all time. How they did it was something of a fascination but what they took sent shockwaves through the book and antiquities world.

A total of 240 books and manuscripts were stolen, including first edition works by Galileo, Leonardo da Vinci, and Sir Isaac Newton, among many others. The total value of the books came in around £2.5million making it the largest book robbery on British soil.

When police arrived on the scene the next morning, they were stunned by the brazenness of the robbery and how it was pulled off. Soon enough, they realised they were dealing with no ordinary robbers.

Mission impossible

On that cold and wet winter's night, a group of thieves put their masterplan into action. As if part of a military operation, they cut a hole through a perimeter fence then scaled the side of the large warehouse using the drainpipe. When they got to the top of the building, they kept lookout across the yards below to make sure they were not spotted.

From there, they crawled across the corrugated metal roof to one of the many fibreglass skylights that littered the rooftop. They cut through the fibreglass with a specialised cutting tool and removed a section big enough to drop through.

The height from the skylight to the floor of the warehouse was over 50 feet so they attached ropes to the fixtures of the skylights and lowered themselves to the floor. They did all of this without tripping alarms or being seen by the extensive CCTV on site.

They had carefully avoided tripping any sensors that were placed by the doors of the building and spent the next five hours searching through various packing cases to get what they had come for.

Using patience, strength, and criminal intelligence, they managed to sneak out 240 rare books and manuscripts in tote bags found in other parcels. 16 large bags of books were lifted by using the ropes as a pulley system to file them through the gap in the skylight.

Content with their haul, they carefully made their way back up the skylight, across the roof, dropped down to the ground below and snuck back through the hole in the perimeter fence – while carrying 16 heavy bags full of books.

First breakthrough

We know how they did it but how was it planned? How did they manage to pull it off without tripping any sensors and avoid being seen on security cameras? The detective on scene that morning posited the same questions, and so began a three year investigation into the theft.

The books belonged to three separate dealers, Alessandro Bisello Bado and one other from Italy, and Michael Kuhn from Berlin, Germany. They had combined their shipments and sent them off to California via Heathrow Airport.

When Alessandro was informed of the robbery he almost fainted but immediately jumped on a plane to London to find out what had gone down. He and the other dealers couldn't make sense of it. Did the thieves want the books for themselves? Were they stealing to order? Were the books the real target?

At first, London detectives assumed the theft may have been part of an insurance scam but they were able to track the thieves across London, and there were a lot of them. On the night of the robbery, the two acrobatic thieves, Daniel David and Victor Opariuc, executed their plan but they were not alone.

Positioned at the edge of the industrial estate was the driver who acted as a lookout, to make sure that no alarms had been tripped or that no police were on to them. By the end of the investigation, 12 men were involved in the robbery. The Frontier Forwarding customs warehouse had been staked out many weeks prior.

The case was escalated to detective inspector Andy Durham of the Metropolitan Specialist

Crime Squad. He and officer David Ward watched 70 hours' worth of CCTV footage from the roadways around Feltham and the estate, and it was then they made the first breakthrough.

Romanian gang

A blue Renault hatchback pulled up near the industrial estate and two men exited the car and headed towards the Frontier Forwarding warehouse. The third man drove off and parked up next to the perimeter fence, as if nothing was untoward. A second car was later suspected to be involved.

The investigation team managed to identify the two cars used, and insurance records showed they belonged to people of Romanian descent, despite having false paperwork. At around the same time, two weeks after the robbery, Romania's chief prosecutor for organised crime, Alina Albu, received a phone call.

The unidentified caller told her about a cache of rare books that had been stolen from a warehouse in London which had ended up in Romania. Assuming it to be a joke, Alina searched online and discovered the story of the theft in Feltham, realising it was true, she called her team in.

Head of organised crime investigations in Romania, Tiberius Manea, put together a team to try and crack the case. They reached out to Durham and Ward in London and put together a joint task force to investigate the theft. It seemed the theft had been part of the Romanian organised crime world.

The book dealers had already put the word out to other dealers through the trade body Antiquarian Booksellers Association. But it didn't always help as many book thieves were known to remove many identifying features before selling them on.

The Bruiser

Realising they were dealing with professional thieves, Durham looked at other warehouse thefts across London and discovered similarities to many others stretching back through the previous year. They discovered that rare book theft had been on the increase since the 2000s, mostly due to international buyers and the reach of the internet.

Evidence shared between the two countries uncovered a link to an infamous Romanian crime family with connections to notorious criminal Cristi 'The Bruiser' Huiduma, whose real name was Gavril Popinciuc. The gang were known to have previously stolen art which was destroyed when they felt the law closing in.

Because of this, the investigation had to tread carefully as they didn't want millions of pounds of irreplaceable books to be burned. The international team of investigators met five times over the next two years to share information and plan the arrest of many co-conspirators.

They knew that Popinciuc headed the organised crime family with Cristian Ungureanu, and they worked out how the organisation was run but they didn't know who else was involved. They needed the so-called foot soldiers to be arrested at the same time to avoid the books being destroyed.

After two years of surveillance and evidence-building, the international investigation made its move. On 25th June 2019, in the early hours of the morning, over 300 officers in England, Netherlands, Italy, and Romania, carried out 45 different raids at various properties, all executed at the same time.

The secret compartment

By the late morning, the investigation had 15 men in custody who were linked to the Romanian crime family and the theft. In January 2020, Ungureanu was arrested in Turin, Italy. By the Autumn of 2020, 13 men were charged with various commercial burglaries across the UK including the Feltham book theft, 12 pleaded guilty.

But the investigation was missing one important aspect – where were the books? Fortunately, in

September 2020, just two weeks before the gang were sentenced, Romanian police were tipped off about a rural property in the north of the country.

They raided the building and uncovered a secret compartment in a cement pit. There, amidst the dust and stale air, were bags and packages containing all but four of the 240 items stolen. When dealer Alessandro found out his books had been recovered, he almost fainted again, for it was unheard of in the stolen art and antiquities world.

By the end of 2020, 12 men including the two acrobatic thieves Daniel David and Victor Opariuc, and gang leaders Ungureanu and Popinciuc were sentenced to various prison terms totalling 48 years. Most were convicted on DNA evidence found at the crime scenes or on the stolen goods.

But questions still remained that have never been answered. The one that always stands out the most is how did the gang know the books would be there on that particular night? Police looked at possible insider knowledge but found no evidence that anyone at the warehouse was involved.

The suspicion fell on the trade fair in California, and any research that had been carried out around it. It may have been possible for the gang to have seen what was to be sold at the fair, track down where it was coming from, and where it would be in transit before arriving there.

Beside that theory there has never been any evidence to suggest exactly how they knew – or how they were going to sell the books. Though there were pricey and incredibly rare, they would have been difficult to sell, even on the black market, as the book world would have known about the theft.

If they had a private buyer set up and were stealing to order then the sale never went ahead. Could there be a secret unidentified book collector out there somewhere who put in an 'order' with the gang? Maybe.

For Alessandro and the other dealers, having most of their books returned to them was something of a miracle – a testament to the hard work of an international investigatory team who never gave up hope.

Bow Cinema Axeman

During the Golden Age of movies, a cinema attendant took an axe to his manager and eloped with a suitcase full of money, in a tale of premeditated murder, historical horrors, and a fake death.

London was at the heart of the burgeoning cinema business in the 1930s, and the Borough of Tower Hamlets was packed full of them, as business owners realised the opportunity that could be afforded to them.

The areas of Bow and Mile End within Tower Hamlets were once home to no less than 33 cinemas with many of the independent ones no longer active, most destroyed in the Second World War and rebuilt as residential property.

One such cinema was the Bow Palace Cinema, sometimes known as the Eastern Palace Cinema due to its heritage. Originally a pub built in 1855, it became the Eastern Empire Theatre in 1892, before becoming the Palace Theatre from 1899 to 1917.

In 1923, it was redeveloped and became home to the Bow Palace Cinema, though many still referred to it as the Eastern. At the time it was taken over by businessman and movie-lover Dudley Henry Hoard and his wife Maisie – until they were brutally attacked by one of their employees.

John Stockwell

By 1934, the cinema was in full swing, taking advantage of the wave of early British and American movies. 19-year-old John Frederick Stockwell was employed as one of the many cinema attendants that helped usher in the crowds and sell tickets.

But John was suddenly tempted into thievery by the amount of money the cinema was taking. On an average weekend, the cinema was reeling in £100, approximately £7,500 in today's money.

John's father, also named John Stockwell, was killed in the First World War, just months after John Junior's birth. Growing up without a father during the fallout of the war was hard enough but his mother died when he was a toddler and John was ultimately raised in various orphanages.

He ended up spending a majority of his childhood in the care of the Salvation Army and their homes. At first, when he got the job at the cinema, he was ecstatic. He was able to watch new films as they were released and expand his social circle as he was friendly with the cinema-goers.

Yet, that life of hardship being raised with no family and little to no money was grinding him down. Surely there must be another way to live well? With that in mind, he began noting how much money the cinema was taking, and for want of a better phrase – finally gave into temptation.

The axeman cometh

Over the weekend of 4th to 5th August 1934, John developed his plan and began to look at where the cinema's takings were being collected. Each night, the money was put into a safe and after each weekend was put into a suitcase by the owner Dudley, for transportation to the local bank.

On the morning of Tuesday 7th August 1934, Dudley was about to leave with the suitcase of money after a bumper weekend when there was a knock at the door. He opened it to find John standing outside who immediately pushed the doors open and entered the cinema.

John wasn't supposed to be working that day and Dudley knew right away that something was wrong. When John – who hadn't tried to disguise himself – attempted to remove the suitcase from the building, he got into a fight with Dudley.

Desperately needing the money and believing it to be the start of a better life, John removed a fire axe he had hidden in his long coat, stormed back into the foyer and hit Dudley over the head with the blade end.

As Dudley fell to the ground, John hit Maisie in the head and she collapsed in a heap. Realising Dudley was still alive, John hit him in the head with the axe another thirteen times, fracturing his skull and killing him instantly.

John then made off with the suitcase, believing both of them to be dead. When the cleaners arrived in the late morning, they walked into the scene of a bloodbath. Dudley was lying in a pool of blood with his head split open and Maisie had seemingly suffered the same fate – until she was found to be alive.

Eagle-eyed holidaymakers

Emergency services arrived at the cinema within minutes as no such crime had been so brazenly committed for many years in Bow. Maisie was rushed to hospital where surgeons managed to keep her alive. Unfortunately for Dudley, it was too late, as he had died at the scene.

Police intricately searched the building and discovered a bloody axe behind the curtains on the stage. Along one of the walls they found a bloody fingerprint that belonged to the killer but with no other witnesses, they needed motive.

Maisie regained consciousness shortly after noon and confirmed with police that the motive was robbery. Even though John worked for the cinema, Maisie could not identify her attacker and said he was a boy in his late teens.

It appeared the mysterious axeman had eloped without a trace but John had another plan in place to disappear for good and it would lead to his downfall. Three days after the murder, John travelled to the coastal town of Lowestoft, 125 miles northeast of Bow.

On the morning of 10th August, Lowestoft police received a suicide letter that was found on Lowestoft beach. The letter was signed by John as J. F. Stockwell and he confessed to Dudley's murder along with the theft.

Though initially not a suspect due to the day of the murder being his day off, John was now prime suspect number one, except it appeared he had taken his own life. When details of the letter were released to the press the same day, some eagle-eyed Lowestoft holidaymakers reported an unusual sight.

Victim of his own stupidity

The same morning the note had been received, various holidaymakers saw a young man place a pile of neatly folded clothes on the golden sandy shoreline, despite already wearing clothes. Nothing was thought of it, until the confession letter was heard of on the news.

Police were directed to the pile of clothes the same afternoon, where they found items belonging to John, in addition to his watch and Post Office savings book – with his name on it. It appeared John's plan was to trick the police into believing he had taken his own life by walking into the sea.

He probably didn't expect that Lowestoft holidaymakers were as eagle-eyed as those elsewhere. When police found out that John had walked away from the beach and not into the sea, a nationwide manhunt went into effect.

The next day on the 14th, John checked into the Metropolitan Hotel in Great Yarmouth, ten miles up the coast. He gave a fake name and his address as Luton, Hertfordshire. When John went up to his room, the hotel manager became suspicious as there was no Luton in Hertfordshire, it was in fact in Bedfordshire.

The hotel had already received word of the manhunt of a young man who may have been in and around Great Yarmouth. The hotel manager believed that John fitted the description of the killer, and combined with the address mistake, called in the police.

Death sentence

When John walked out of the hotel just minutes later, the manager thought he may have spooked him but it turned out that John wanted to go on a shopping spree. Police were made aware of his location and they watched him enter many shops, stocking up on pricey goods.

When John arrived back at the hotel, Great Yarmouth police were waiting for him and arrested him on sight. Knowing the game was up, John didn't resist arrest. He was interviewed in Great Yarmouth where he confessed and was driven back down to London to face charges.

Two months later on 22nd October, after a very public trial, John pleaded guilty to murder but he had a story already laid out. When John had arrived at the cinema that fateful morning, he claimed that he told Dudley he'd left personal money in the building and was going to retrieve it.

He believed his personal money was in the suitcase of cash and when he tried to look inside, Dudley stopped him, resulting in an axe to the head. Yep, the court didn't believe him either and he was ultimately convicted of murder.

The fact that John had taken an axe to the cinema in the first instance and planned his fake death meant it was a pre-meditated murder, and as such received the harshest sentence – death.

Horrors of the past

On 14th November 1934, John was led to the gallows at Pentonville Prison and had no final words to say. He was executed by hanging that same morning. A total of 120 men between 1902 and 1961 were executed at Pentonville Prison, and it remains one of Britain's most notorious execution sites.

For Maisie, justice had been served, and though she didn't make a full recovery from her injuries, she lived out the rest of her life as best she could. Her husband, Dudley, had been buried three days after John was captured.

Due to the tragedy that had befallen the cinema, it was rebuilt as an Art Deco style building to become the Regal Cinema. As fate would have it, the building was bombed by Germans during the Second World War.

The Regal was rebuilt again and reopened in 1947 before ultimately closing its doors for good in 1958. Built upon the ruins of bombings and bloody murder, the site has been home to various residential buildings, with many tenants unaware of the horrors of the past.

The Freddy Krueger Killer

A man inspired by horror movies went on a rampage that left four dead and two injured, in a tragic case that laid the blame at the feet of those put in place to protect the public.

Though many horror movies are said to incite violence, they are no less inciting than watching a 24-hour news cycle. Many violent people who it is said were influenced by horror movies already have something wrong within them that causes them to lash out, and none more so than in the case of David Gonzalez.

Between the 15th and 17th September 2004, David, aged 24, went on a killing spree wearing a hockey mask similar to the one Jason Vorhees wears in the Friday the 13th films. Though wearing a hockey mask, he later claimed that he was similar to Freddy Krueger from Nightmare on Elm Street.

The killing spree was a result of the failure of the system to protect David from himself and others, something that will become evidently clear shortly. David stocked up on various drugs, took a knife from his mother's kitchen and walked out the house intent on killing.

So intent on killing that he was aiming to become the most notorious serial killer in history. He wrote about his experiences in letter form calling himself Zippy. When he was committed to the maximum security Broadmoor psychiatric hospital, the doctors said he was the sickest patient they had ever seen and that the killing spree could have been prevented.

Not taken seriously

Born in 1980 in Surrey to an English mother, Lesley, and Spanish father, he was raised in a good household and educated at a private school in Woking. His parents split up when he was six, and his mother remarried his stepfather Steven Harper shortly after.

He left school with good grades and was known to be an expert at chess but from the age of 17, David required mental health care. For reasons unknown, he was found to be a troubled teenager who had severe psychological problems.

By the age of 24, he was unable to find work and was using drugs. He spent most of his time playing video games and watching horror movies. There were a number of unusual incidents before his killing spree where he required professional help but was never given it.

During his late teens and early twenties, his mother, Lesley, contacted authorities on multiple occasions but was told each time that a crisis would have to occur before David could get the help he needed.

She even wrote a letter to her MP and social services asking why her son would have to commit a serious offence before being taken seriously. In the letter, she said, '*does David have to murder someone before he can get the treatment he so badly needs?*' Neither the MP nor social services replied.

In 2003, a year before the murders, David himself wrote a letter to his GP that said he needed help and was trying to cope with life as a normal human being but unable to succeed in doing so.

In the letter, regarding previous mental health help he had received in 1998 when he was 18, he wrote, '*I really need to go to hospital voluntarily and receive treatment under the care of the doctors before my mental state gets worse.*'

'Please help me'

The letter continued, '*please, please help me, this is very urgent. I really would appreciate if you would help me improve as I am in a desperate situation.'* And despite his doctor making an appointment with him, David was never admitted to hospital.

After the murders, Lesley said she knew something bad was going to happen but everywhere she turned, her calls for help were turned down. The day before the killing spree, Steven was sitting in a car outside the family home when David ran out the front door naked.

It was around the time that Steven was about to drive to work which meant schoolchildren were on their way to school in their droves. David had run out into the street and was seen naked by many children. Steven drove after him but lost him in the streets around their home.

He phoned Lesley at her job and told her that David was running around town naked. She told him to go home and wait for him but David was already there when he got back. He was standing naked in the front room and answered Steven in a deep growly voice.

Steven then did the only thing he could have done in that situation – phoned the police. On the phone he mentioned that David may be suffering from paranoid schizophrenia and was not taking any medication for it as he hadn't been diagnosed yet. While he was on the phone, David began punching himself in the head, giving himself a black eye. He later said that he wanted to hurt himself as much as possible, to degrade his body and harm his flesh. He even threw himself down the stairs three times to break his bones.

Despite exposing himself in public, calls from a worried stepfather, clear instances of self-harm, the police never came, and three days later, four people would be dead because of it.

Killing spree begins

The next day, Wednesday 15th September 2004, David jumped on a train to Portsmouth and departed the train at Portsmouth and Southsea station. He walked the short distance to Hilsea where he saw an elderly couple out with their dog.

He approached 61-year-old Peter King and his wife and told them in no uncertain terms that he was going to kill them. David pulled the knife from his pocket and attacked the couple but Peter managed to fight him off, and David ran away from the scene. Peter and his wife were the lucky ones.

David caught a train to Southwick, a few miles east of Brighton, where he departed the train and went on the hunt for another victim. As he went on the hunt, he put on a hockey mask like Jason Vorhees, and found 73-year-old Marie Harding walking alone on a footpath.

He approached her from behind and stabbed her in the back before cutting her throat and running off with her purse. Police spent the next 48 hours searching the area around the crime scene and looking for any witnesses of which there were none. The hockey mask was found nearby and later tested positive for David's DNA.

Unknown to police, David had caught a train back up to London and went back home with no-one questioning where he had been. A day later and with no sign of the law closing in, he went on the lookout for his next victims, in an attempt to become one of the worst serial killers in the history of Britain.

Tottenham murder spree

At 5am on Friday 17th September, he caught a train to Tottenham, North London. There, on Tottenham High Road, David walked up behind 46-year-old Kevin Molloy and stabbed him in the face with knives he had stolen from a department store the day before. When Kevin retaliated, David stabbed him in the chest and neck, killing him instantly.

Less than two hours later in nearby Hornsby, 59-year-old Koumis Constantinou was lying in bed when he awoke to find David standing over him. Koumis was stabbed many times before his wife walked back into the room and managed to fight David off, who then ran out the house.

Fortunately, Koumis survived the attack but was left with life-changing injuries. Less than 15 minutes later, David broke into the home of Derek and Jean Robinson in Highgate. They were just waking up for the day when David stabbed them both in the throat, killing them instantly.

After receiving multiple reports of a madman on the loose, police descended on the area around Tottenham and ultimately arrested David at Tottenham Court Road Tube station, where he was seen by commuters covered in blood. He had also been spotted by a painter and decorator leaving the Robinson's home with a knife.

During the attacks, David had taken lots of drugs, which he claimed made the murders feel *'orgasmic.'* It was already clear that if he wasn't arrested he would have gone on to kill as many as he could. During the trial and found in subsequent letters written by him he claimed the murders to have been *'one of the best things I've done in my life.'*

In each of the letters he referred to himself as Zippy, which was a nickname he'd had since childhood for unknown reasons. He also claimed that he wanted to get professional help before the murders but no-one would help him. If they had then he said the murders would never have happened.

Freddy Krueger

At the trial it materialised that he was inspired to kill by some of his favourite horror characters, most notably Freddy Krueger and Jason Vorhees. Although he had worn the Jason Vorhees mask when he killed Marie Harding, he likened himself to Freddy Krueger and would sometimes tape knives to his fingers and pretend to be the character.

Before his trial, David was kept at the maximum security Broadmoor psychiatric hospital. While there, he attempted to bite through an artery in his arm, in an incident so severe that doctors said they had never seen someone bite themselves with such ferocity.

And then, despite his obvious mental health condition and danger to himself, his plea of guilty by diminished responsibility was rejected. The prosecution made him out to be a calculating psychopath who killed because he was the epitome of evil.

In 2006, in another failure by the system, a jury agreed that David was not mentally ill and found him guilty of four murders as a normal human being. He was handed down six life sentences, four for murder and two for violent assault.

Most disturbed

And yet, despite the courts finding him to be a capable and culpable criminal, David was still imprisoned at Broadmoor. There, the doctors attempting to treat him said that he was the most disturbed patient they had ever seen.

Just one year later, in 2007, after another attempt at biting himself to death, David slashed his wrists with parts of a broken CD case and died of massive blood loss. His suicide in a maximum security hospital raised even further questions about he had been treated and not treated.

It's no surprise that after David's suicide, an inquiry was held, which found the Surrey and Borders NHS Foundation Trust lacking in their support of someone with severe mental health issues.

The trust apologised to David's victims and their families and implemented new recommendations and regulations when it came to treating mental health patients both before and after a family member reports that they need help.

But for the families of the dead and injured, the inquiry had come too late, and their lives were forever altered by a man believing himself to be Freddy Krueger, someone who with the right help could have got the treatment he needed to have never committed murder.

The Tale of The Man They Could Not Hang

An Englishman sentenced to death was led up the steps of the gallows to be executed, but despite multiple attempts, he dodged the noose, leading to a strange tale of murder and luck.

I n 1884, the town of Babbacombe, in Devon, England, was shocked to its core when a wealthy woman named Emma Ann Whitehead Keyse was brutally murdered. She had been beaten before having her throat cut and her body set on fire.

Her employee, a footman named John Lee – as he was the only man in the house at the time – was arrested and ultimately charged with her murder. Born in 1865 and aged just 20 at the time of Keyse' death, the circumstantial evidence against him was convincing.

A bloodied knife was found in the drawer beside Lee's bed which would have been convincing enough except Lee was covered in blood. He claimed he had cut his arm after smashing a window trying to save Keyse from the fire.

As he had previous run-ins with the law, usually to do with theft, police arrested him and took him down to the local station immediately. He had also been overheard threatening to burn the Keyse's home to the ground.

The evidence was enough to convict him and he was sentenced to death. But when it came to hang him at the gallows, it seemed lady luck had come to visit.

The gallows

On 5th February 1885, Lee was found guilty of murder. From the moment he was arrested, to the steps up the gallows, Lee protested his innocence.

"The reason I am so calm, is that I trust in the Lord, and he knows that I am innocent." – John Lee at his trial in 1885.

It was then, with curious fortune that they couldn't hang him. A few days after his sentencing, on a wet Winter's morning, Lee had a sack placed on his head and was led from the cell to the outside gallows.

He was guided up the steps to the trapdoor where a noose was placed around his neck. Despite pleading innocence, Lee acknowledged that he was about to hang, and in some ways had come to accept his fate.

The executioner that day was James Berry, a Yorkshireman who carried out 131 hangings in his seven years as executioner. Out of the 131, he hung five women, along with a man named William Bury, who many suspected of being Jack the Ripper.

In the 1892 book 'My Experiences as an Executioner' that Berry wrote, there was one case that stood out above all the rest; John Lee. For when Berry pulled the lever to release the trapdoor, the lever wouldn't budge.

Failed execution

Wardens took over and tried to kick the trapdoor out from under Lee's feet, risking their own death in the process, but it still wouldn't move. After several minutes of trying to force the trapdoor, they gave up and moved Lee to one side.

Without Lee on the gallows, the equipment was tested thoroughly. Berry pulled the lever and the trap door opened with ease, exactly how it should have done. After what seemed like a lifetime to Lee, he was led back up the steps and the noose placed around his neck.

Berry leaned in, took hold of the lever and – the trapdoor didn't budge. On a final attempt, not only did the door remain closed, but Berry, with all his strength, had managed to bend the lever and warp it out of position.

The medical officer, who was present at all executions, decided enough was enough and put an end to the execution. But when Lee was led away from the gallows, the trapdoor dropped open all by itself.

Naturally, in Victorian times, the first theory was witchcraft, that either Lee himself was involved in the practice or that someone had been spiritually assisting him from the outside.

The second more plausible theory was that other prisoners had tampered with the gallows in secret. However, the truth was far more normal.

When the story got out to the press, there was uproar among the public, which led to Queen Victoria asking the home secretary to intervene. Sir William Harcourt commuted Lee's sentence to life imprisonment, on the basis of damage caused by a judicial mishap.

Harcourt ordered an investigation into the failed execution and the equipment was taken away. A gallows trapdoor is supported by bolts which release when the lever is pulled. One of the bolts was an eighth of an inch misaligned which had held the trapdoor up.

John Lee

Lee remained in prison for 22 years, continuing to protest his innocence. After petitioning various home secretaries, he was released as a free man in 1907. He sold his story to the press, gave some lectures on the botched execution, and then disappeared without a trace.

From around 1912, there is no record of what happened to Lee or where he went. For a hundred years, historians and researchers have attempted to trace his whereabouts and ultimate death with varying conclusions coming to the fore.

One claimed he died on Australia's Gold Coast in 1918, while another claimed he went to Canada and became a gold prospector, going on to have a successful life. Another theory was that he went to America, suffered from depression, and took his own life in 1930. Yet another claimed he died in England during the Second World War.

The most evidential story goes that he fled on a passenger liner from Southampton to New York in 1912, leaving his new wife and their child behind. He eloped with his barmaid mistress, Adelina Gibbs, who posed as his wife, getting them entry into the United States.

As recently as 2009, it was suggested the Milwaukee grave of a man named John Abbotskerswell was in fact John Lee, having changed his name on arrival to America. Date of death; 19th March 1945.

Lady luck

It is with curious wonder that if John Lee was innocent of the murder of Emma Keyse, then the trapdoor not opening was a sign from a higher power, as some have come to believe. But what if John Lee really was innocent? Who killed Emma Keyse?

More recently, a new suspect has surfaced, under the name of Reginald Gwynne Templer, a local solicitor who was known to Keyse. At the time, rumours were circulating of a gentlemen (Templer) having extra marital relations with a servant in the house named Elizabeth.

In the book 'The Man They Could Not Hang' it was concluded the two had been fraternising in the house and disturbed Keyse who had come down to investigate, resulting in her bloody murder.

When Templer died many years later, another solicitor at the funeral claimed to Templer's sons they had just buried the secret of the Babbacombe murder. Yet, despite the many books, blog posts, and tales over the years, there has never been any solid evidence to back it up.

In 2018, the noose said to have been around Lee's neck was auctioned and purchased by the

Gloucestershire Crime Through Time museum for a little over £3,000 (GBP).

We may never know who really killed Emma Keyse, whether John Lee was falsely claiming innocence or if someone else had killed her. It is certain, however, that Lee survived the hangman's noose by a miraculous turn of luck. His story continues to fascinate and intrigue to this day.

Nude in the Nettles

A strange phone call leads to the discovery of a woman's body on the North York Moors, but for over 40 years, her identity and death remain a mystery, and one of England's oddest unsolved cold cases.

Orth Yorkshire, in England, is home to the North York Moors National Park, with rolling green landscapes and windy fields. Nestled in the Hambleton District of the North York Moors is Sutton Bank, a hill with extensive views over the Vale of York and the Vale of Mowbray.

Close by is Roulston Scar, an Iron Age hill fort built in the 5th Century, a place of historical interest where the Battle of Old Byland took place, in which the Scots mounted an attack and defeated the forces of King Edward II.

Fifteen Centuries later, on the morning of 28th August 1981, Constable John Jeffries of Ripon

Police had arrived at the station to start his shift. Shortly after, he received a phone call from a well-spoken man with a trace of a local Yorkshire accent.

He said, '*near Scawton Moor House, you will find a decomposed body among the willow herbs.*' Unsure what to make of it, Jeffries asked for the man's name and address. To which the reply was, '*I cannot divulge this information for reasons of national security*', before hanging up.

Before the man had hung up, he had provided detailed instructions on where they could find the body. When Jeffries took it to his superiors, they suggested the onus was on him to find it. He walked up to Sutton Bank, and there among the willow herbs, he found human bones.

Remains

The search hadn't been easy, Jeffries had scoured the area for an hour before discovering the remains, packed tightly into the sprawling bushes around the area. Detective Chief Superintendent Strickland Carter was called to the scene with his CID squad, who mounted a large operation.

They spent almost half a day removing the willow herbs and shrubbery from around the bones and used a team to scour Sutton Bank in search for further remains. Then, near to the top of the hill, close to Scawton Moor House, beside a country road, they found a decomposed body.

With the Yorkshire Ripper, Peter Sutcliffe, having been arrested seven months earlier, murder was fresh on Carter's mind. Though Sutcliffe had been active in Yorkshire, he was not known to have ventured to the area around Sutton Bank.

An investigation discovered the body was that of a female and that she would have been nude at the time of her death, suggesting foul play. But there seemed to be no knife marks on the bones nor had her skull been crushed by a blunt object. There were no clothes nearby, she had no jewellery, and no identifying piece of evidence.

Due to the decomposition of the body, and the rate the willow herbs had grown up around it, it was suggested she had died at least one year earlier. This was confirmed when they removed the body and found a yogurt pot underneath her, with a sell-by-date of 1979.

Sutton Bank Body

Even though Sutton Bank was popular with hikers and families on picnics, the body had remained undisturbed for nearly two years. Due to the Ripper case being fresh in the memories of the detectives, they made sure to thoroughly detail the crime scene, with hundreds of photos.

As soon as the media got hold of the story, the mystery of the Nude in the Nettles was born. Despite nettles and willow herbs being two very different species of plants, an eager reporter may have been close to the police boundary, saw some nettles nearby and came up with the name.

It's remarkable how many names and monikers of serial killers, cold cases, unidentified bodies, and other crimes, are given to us by newspapers and the media – mostly to sell more copies or get more views on a website.

Some more conservative newspapers ran with *Sutton Bank Body*, though it was the Nude in the Nettles that drew more people in. Due to the fact she was nude, police suspected she had been murdered but had no evidence to go on, or motive.

More importantly, the identity of the woman was a mystery. The only link they had to the body was the mystery phone caller who led them there. But before the days of phone tracking, whether the man was simply a good Samaritan or someone involved in the murder, we'll never know.

Reconstruction

Due to the media attention, the profile of the case was lifted and the public became invested. This gave local police the impetus to hold press conferences in which they appealed to the public if they knew of any woman who had disappeared in the past two years.

Unsurprisingly they were overrun with phone calls and messages to the local station with no solid leads materialising. Detective Carter had recently read an Egyptian article where scientists had reconstructed the face of an ancient Mummy, and thought it was a good idea.

Though facial reconstruction had been around since 1883, it was mostly used in archaeology. It wasn't until 1962 that scientist Wilton Krogman popularised it in the field of forensics. The subsequent facial reconstruction of the Nude in the Nettles was a landmark moment in UK forensics.

But it didn't help the case, even after releasing the image to the public. During the investigation, some items of clothing, including underwear, were found hanging on a tree less than a mile away, but again – there was no evidence to suggest the clothing belonged to the woman.

One possible identity for the victim was an escaped prisoner named Geraldine Crawley, who escaped from Askham Grange prison in 1979. But when they made the name public, Geraldine herself sent a letter to the police with her fingerprints claiming she was alive – eventually leading to her recapture.

4601

In 2012, after advances in forensic testing and DNA technology had reached a good enough level, the body of the unidentified woman was exhumed. She had been buried in a council cemetery, under a small headstone displaying '4601', the identifier of her position among the dead.

A full DNA profile was able to be extracted which gave investigators the opportunity to compare the results with potential families, and to add the profile to the national DNA database. Despite comparing it to people who claimed the woman was a family member, there were no matches.

With the advances of genealogy websites and larger DNA databases, the police are still hopeful that one day, the woman and the cause of her death may be identified.

The police have since confirmed that there were no missing person reports that matched the description of the woman at the time she had died. It remains a mystery why no one would have reported her missing unless something darker was afoot.

Unsolved

The location the body was found was close to a by-road heading to the popular tourist town of Scarborough, a place visited by people from all over the country. It was deemed a possibility, that the woman was killed elsewhere, taken by car along a country road near to a tourist town, and left in a patch of willow herb close to the road.

And what about Peter Sutcliffe? On 4th April 1979, Sutcliffe killed 19-year-old Josephine Whitaker on Savile Park Moor in Halifax, 70 miles away from Sutton Bank.

Later that year, on 1st September, he murdered 20-year-old Barbara Leach and dumped her body under a pile of bricks in Bradford. He killed some of his victims with a screwdriver by stabbing them in the neck and abdomen, parts of the body that wouldn't leave marks on the bones.

He murdered at least 13 women between the ages of 16 and 47, an age bracket the Nude in the Nettles fell into. He mostly killed prostitutes, which may have explained why no one had reported the woman missing, as she may have been estranged from her family.

However, Sutcliffe never spoke of the unidentified body on Sutton Bank and was never questioned about it. Police at the time were just happy to have caught him and taken him off the streets. Perhaps their insistence the mystery caller was the killer took them away from the Sutcliffe possibility.

A frustrating aspect of the case materialised in the days after the body was found. In 1979, a local horse-rider had passed the patch where the body was later found and noticed a terrible smell. He was going to return later that day to investigate but fell off his horse and broke his leg.

He forgot about the incident until he watched the news two years later. Had he found the body at the time, then there would have been a strong possibility the case would have been solved. As it is, the Nude in the Nettles remains Yorkshire's most mysterious unsolved cold case.

The World's End Murderer

Angus Sinclair was a dangerous predator capable of sinking to the depths of depravity, convicted of four murders and linked to many more, he was one of Britain's worst serial killers.

On 20th November 1978, the body of 17-year-old Mary Gallacher was found on waste ground near a footbridge at Barnhill Railway Station, in Glasgow, Scotland. She would come to be known as a victim of one of Britain's worst serial killers but it took another 23 years to bring the killer to justice.

The judge who first sentenced Angus Sinclair told him he was '*a dangerous predator capable of sinking to the depths of depravity.*' No truer words were spoken about the man who would become known as The World's End Murderer.

In 1961 at the age of just 16, Sinclair killed his seven-year-old neighbour Catherine Reehill. She was visiting family in Glasgow's Woodlands when she went to a nearby shop only to never return. Sinclair lured her to his family home where he raped and strangled her to death.

Even at such a young age, his callousness was well known. After killing Catherine, he threw her body down the stairs then called an ambulance and claimed she had fallen in an accident. The police saw right through his evil ways and arrested him for murder.

Unfortunately for his future victims, he was able to strike a plea deal where he was sentenced to a lesser charge of culpable homicide. He was released six years into a ten year sentence and was allowed to kill again – and again.

World's End

Upon his release, in his early twenties, he got married and had a son, nothing was seemingly untoward for a short while. On 15th October 1977, two teenagers named Helen Scott and Christine Eadie were seen leaving the World's End Pub on Edinburgh's Royal Mile.

The next day, Christine's naked body was discovered by hikers in East Lothian. Helens' body was found over six miles away in a corn field. They had been raped, abused, beaten, and strangled to death with their bodies left in the open without any attempt to hide them.

The murders of Helen and Christine would later become known as the World's End Murders, and Sinclair; The World's End Murderer. Due to the media running with the story in a big way, some witnesses suggested they had seen the girls with two men that night.

This claim was backed up by police who said that both girls had been tied with different knotting methods. As a possible link between two men was made, the investigation garnered widespread attention and over 13,000 witness statements were taken.

500 suspects were drawn up but no culprit was identified at the time. At the time of the World's End murders, the police had failed to make a connection with four other women who had been found and killed in a similar fashion throughout the same year.

Murder spree

A cold case investigation discovered that during 1977, six young women had disappeared after nights out across the central belt of Scotland, which is generally referred to as a fifty mile stretch from Glasgow to Edinburgh.

Along with Helen and Christine, four other victims were later linked to Sinclair. 37-year-old Frances Barker disappeared outside her home in Maryhill in July 1977 after getting a taxi home from visiting family in Parkhead.

When her body was found at a waste ground, 44-year-old sex offender Thomas Young was arrested and convicted of her murder. At every step of the way, he protested his innocence, and it wouldn't be until his death in prison in 2014 that Sinclair was linked to Barker's murder.

20-year-old Glasgow brewery worker Anna Kenny disappeared in August 1977 after leaving the Hurdy Gurdy bar in the city. She was raped and strangled, and her decomposed remains were found two years later in Skipness, Argyll.

In October 1977, 36-year-old Hilda McAuley was raped, beaten and found dumped on wasteland in Langbank, Renfrewshire. In December, 23-year-old Agnes Cooney disappeared after a night out at the Clada social club in Govanhill. She was tortured, stabbed 26 times and dumped on moorland at Caldercruik. Sinclair was later linked to all four murders but justice was decades away.

Escaping justice

In May of 1978, the investigation was scaled down. The World's End murders, at least for a while, fell into dark Scottish legend. As the investigation dwindled, Sinclair saw opportunity to kill again. His inability to control his urges would lead to the 1978 killing of 17-year-old Mary Gallacher on a footpath in Glasgow.

She was abducted under cover of darkness, raped and strangled to death with a ligature made from the leg of her trousers before her throat was cut for good measure. She was found dead on a dumping ground, nude from the waist down, exposed to the elements.

Sinclair would not be convicted of that particular murder until 2001, when DNA matching cold cases connected him to the crime. It had remained until then, one of Scotland's most mysterious murders.

The Gallacher murder deepened the divide between Glasgow and Edinburgh as the investigation into her death was not as large as the two Edinburgh murders the year before. It was assumed by some that murders in Glasgow were not deemed as important as those in Edinburgh, due to the poverty and cultural divide between Scotland's two largest cities.

Gallacher's murder led Sinclair to change the way he chose his victims. There had been a witness to her abduction and the police were closing in, albeit to the wrong people but Sinclair turned his attention elsewhere.

Psychologists believed it was the witness that led Sinclair to devise different tactics. Unfortunately, it led him to start preying on children. Between

1978 to 1982, Sinclair raped, sexually abused, or assaulted dozens of young girls in the Glasgow area.

He was arrested in 1982 and pleaded guilty to the rape and sexual assault of 11 girls between the ages of six to 14-years-old. He was sentenced to life in prison for the abuse but it was almost 20 years later that he would be charged with murder.

Operation Trinity

A 2000 cold case review of Mary Gallacher's murder linked Sinclair's DNA to her death, leading to his conviction of her murder in 2001, 23 years later, and getting him another life sentence. In 2004, realising Sinclair may have murdered more, three Scottish police forces came together and formed Operation Trinity, to review all the 1977 murders and hundreds of others before and after.

Forensic experts proved that the other four murders of 1977 showed they had a unique signature belonging to Sinclair. Incidentally, Sinclair had provided his DNA voluntarily while in prison.

It was also claimed he carried out some of the murders with his brother-in-law Gordon Hamilton who died in 1996 before justice could find him. Recent evidence showed that Hamilton was implicit in at least one of the murders.

By 2007, the World's End murders had been attributed to him but the trial was to collapse in an extraordinary miscarriage of justice. Sinclair's lawyers had put forward two special defences, one that included the belief the two girls had consented to sexual intercourse with Sinclair.

The second being that anything that happened after that – the murders – were the actions of Gordon Hamilton. Because there was insufficient evidence to prove any sexual encounter had not been consensual then the judge infamously dismissed the case.

Double jeopardy

The news of the verdict caused mass outcry in Scotland and widespread criticism of the police and justice system. The resulting shift in Scottish Law was felt internationally as the Scottish Parliament managed to legally circumnavigate the double jeopardy law.

It was a law which used to mean that one couldn't be tried for the same crime twice. But in 2011, the Scottish Parliament passed the Double Jeopardy Act 2011. It had made various provisions for circumstances when a person convicted or acquitted of an offence could be newly prosecuted.

As such, in 2014, there was a controversial retrial of the World's End murders, which involved the jury visiting the locations where the bodies were found. Sinclair was then found guilty of Helen and Christine's murders in November 2014.

He was sentenced to life in prison on top of his convictions for abuse and the murder of Mary Gallacher. Sinclair was the first person in Scotland to be given a retrial of the same crimes under the new law. His parole date would have been when he was 108-years-old, meaning he was never going to be released from prison.

Sinclair died of natural causes in HM Prison Glen Ochil on 11th March 2019. He was never charged with the four additional murders of 1977 but they have since been linked to him through DNA evidence and cold case reviews. He killed at least seven people and abused at least 11 more but he had left behind many more deaths in his wake.

The family of Hilda McAuley suffered from a suicide relating to the case. Anna Kenny's parents died young, as did her brother, supposedly due to the stress of losing a family member. Other family members of the dead still hold a grudge against a police investigation they say failed them.

Angus Sinclair was one of Britain's most notorious serial killers, with additional murders linked to him using modern research techniques. Gordon Hamilton, it seemed, managed to get away with murder, but if they had worked together as a pair, it seems certain there are many more victims out there.

Ultimately, for the families of the dead, the monster who took their loved ones is long gone, confined to the corridors of hell for eternity.

Great Coram Street Murder

In Victorian London, a lady of the night was found in her room with her throat slashed, and the door locked from the outside. Read the story of one of the oldest unsolved murders in London.

Great Coram Street, now simply Coram Street, is located one block away from Russell Square Tube Station, in the Bloomsbury area of London. It's an area rich with hotels, hostels, and self-catering apartments, a feature carried over from Victorian times.

On Christmas afternoon, 1872, the landlady of lodgings in Great Coram Street, became concerned when one of her tenants didn't return her calls. She had the door to the room broken down by some burly men, who were met with a horrific sight.

Laying in her bed with her face turned to the ceiling, was 27-year-old penniless London prostitute and wannabe actress, Harriet Buswell. Her throat had been cut from ear to ear, and her bedclothes were stained with blood.

Harriet's death remains one of the oldest unsolved murders in London. Preceding Jack the Ripper by 16 years, the Great Coram Street Murder continues to fascinate both true crime enthusiasts, and those who believe the Ripper may have been around a little earlier.

The Lost Alhambra

Harriet was working at one of the local theatres in London, as a member of the 'corps de ballet', a background dancer, but her dream was to be an actress. Because the theatre paid her a pittance, she resorted to prostitution to pay for her day to day living.

For four weeks prior to her murder, she had managed to secure lodgings with landlady Mrs. Wright at 12 Great Coram Street. Harriet had left her previous landlady of two years for reasons unknown and asked Mrs. Wright if she could have a room for at least a week.

After which, she requested to have an apartment but Mrs. Wright stated she only let out apartments to men. Mrs. Wright was unaware that Harriet would be using the room for nightly encounters with men paying for her services.

On Christmas Eve, Harriet left the lodgings to visit the Alhambra Theatre Bar in Leicester Square, she was wearing a black silk dress, black velvet jacket, and a dark green brigand hat with a red feather. The Alhambra was one of the few bars in London that accepted women without the escort of a man. Once described as the *'greatest place of infamy in all London.'*

The theatre bar burned down in 1882 and was rebuilt but was said to be cursed by debauchery. It was demolished and rebuilt again as the Odeon Cinema. Today, a cocktail bar next to the Odeon, called the Lost Alhambra, has been resurrected, though less infamous than its Victorian roots.

Harriet would frequent the Alhambra on numerous occasions and it became a place to pick up well-to-do men, and some less upstanding men. That night, she caught an omnibus – a horse drawn bus – with two of the barmaids from the Alhambra, along with an unidentified male friend.

The omnibus took them all from Piccadilly Circus to Russell Square, where Harriet stepped off with her male friend. She returned to her lodgings in the late of the night and told Mrs. Wright that she had a gentleman with her.

Harriet had borrowed some money from another tenant to pay her rent and she gave Mrs. Wright a half-sovereign from which to take her rent for the following week. After getting back one shilling, she retreated to her room where the male friend was waiting – and was never seen alive again.

Large enough to put a man's fist in

At 3pm on Christmas afternoon, police were called to Harriet's room, and they reported one of the most horrific crimes they had seen until then. Detective Superintendent Thomson relayed their initial findings to the press:

"The murderer stabbed the poor girl under the left ear, and there is another wound on the left of the wind-pipe large enough to put a man's fist in. The object of the murderer was evidently to possess himself of what trinkets and money the girl possessed, for earrings which she had borrowed to wear were not to be found; and a purse into which she was seen to put the shilling change was also missing."

Spots of blood were found in various places around the room, which led police to believe the killer must have been splattered with Harriet's blood. Her body was taken to St. Giles's Workhouse morgue, and was identified by her brother, who travelled from their home county of Berkshire.

Police tracked down the two barmaids who said that Harriet was in the company of a German-speaking man of high calibre. A fruit shop owner came forward to say he had seen Harriet enter his shop with the man but suspected nothing to be wrong at the time.

The investigation agreed the man must have had blood on his clothing, as the wounds Harriet had received would have sprayed blood in every direction. There were bloodstains in the sink where the killer would have washed his hands.

He also took the time to lock the door to the room behind him as he exited and took the key with him. He was heard by other tenants leaving the building in the early hours of Christmas morning. Descriptions of the man were amalgamated and released to the press and public.

"He is about 23 years of age, 5ft. 9in. high, with neither beard, whiskers, nor moustache, but not having shaved for two or three days, his beard when grown would be rather dark. He has a swarthy complexion, and blotches or pimples on his face. He was dressed in dark clothes and wore a dark brown overcoat down to the knees, billycock hat, and rather heavy boots."

The Wangerland

Two days later, reports were spreading of a male passenger who fitted the description, being spotted at Harwich port, ready to board the Great Eastern route ferry to Rotterdam in the

Netherlands. But police claimed the killer would not have got there in time as his description was sent to the ports as soon as it had been released.

Except, there was a ship in Ramsgate Harbour that flew a German flag, and knowing they were looking for a German-speaking man, police descended on the ship. The Wangerland was a German emigrant ship that was undergoing repairs at the harbour.

Due to the brutality of the murder, the case had spread around England like wildfire, and it became the talk of the country. Knowing they had to find a suspect soon, the police put all their efforts into the German link.

They initially suspected a chemist from the ship named Carl Wohllebe but they needed to have him identified by the witnesses. To fill out the line-up, the police picked some other Germans at random from the ship and put them together.

As the revolving door of witnesses were shown the line-up of Germans, the police were surprised to see that no-one picked Carl. Instead, some pointed the finger to the ship's chaplain, Dr. Gottfried Hessel, as he slightly resembled the killer. Many more ruled him out completely.

But the police needed a suspect. They learned that Hessel had been in London from 23rd December and had a history of fraud and financial crime – which was enough. On 21st January 1873,

Hessel appeared in court, charged with Harriet's wilful murder.

It didn't quite go the way police had intended it too. For starters, Hessel had been ill with bronchitis at the time of the murder and remained in his own hotel room over Christmas. His illness was backed up by his wife and many hotel workers who confirmed he was room-bound, thus giving him an alibi.

The magistrates threw out the case on the basis of the alibis and found Hessel innocent of any wrongdoing, even compensating him for wrongful arrest. The police couldn't see past their belief that the killer was Hessel, and in doing so, may have given time for the real killer to get away.

A Victorian mystery

Though policing was not to the standard it is in today's world, the murder of Harriet Buswell created quite the furore in Victorian London, and every effort was made to catch the killer. It is possible that some witnesses confused German with any other foreign language.

London was the epicentre of 19th Century multiculturalism, and people from all over the world were roaming the streets, looking for their piece of the pie in business or in leisure – or in something darker.

Something horrific occurred at that rundown lodge-house on Great Coram Street over Christmas in 1872. A murder that has remained unsolved for 140 years, despite various attempts to reach into the past and dig for unseen clues.

The spirit of Christmas was strong in London that year, with families coming together to celebrate. But another spirit had come to London at the same time to wreak death and bloody murder on an unsuspecting young woman, who simply aspired to be something greater than the life she was dealt.

It remains unlikely that Hessel was the killer, the alibis were too strong, and his illness too prevalent to have seen him roam the cold streets and decadent bars. The man Harriet brought back to her room may not have been the killer, and someone else may have entered after the man had left.

What really happened to Harriet that night remains a mystery, beyond the evidence of the murder. We may never know who or what violently took her life that Christmas but it appears that someone got away with murder.

The ghost of Harriet was said to have haunted the lodgings for decades afterwards, until the street was rebuilt following the two world wars. But even today, as the bells chime across London, and families celebrate Christmas, the echoes of Harriet's death remain.

The Horrors of Dennis Nilsen

The sickening tale of British serial killer Dennis Nilsen, who killed 15 young men, and dissected some of their remains – before flushing them down the toilet and blocking the sewers with flesh.

Dennis Nilsen is one of Britain's most infamous serial killers. Some see him as the British version of Jeffrey Dahmer and in a lot of ways, the similarities are striking. They both killed gay men and they made their first kill within five months of each other in 1978. Nilsen killed 15, Dahmer killed 17, and they both carried out necrophilia acts upon the bodies of their victims.

Yet, the very nature of their crimes are inherently different. Because of the United Kingdom's different legal system to that of the United States, Dennis Nilsen was sentenced to life, as since 1969, the country no longer carries the death sentence.

Nilsen would request parole hearings for immediate release up until his death in 2018 when he died of natural causes. He reached out from within his cell with now banned autobiographies and interviews to sate the appetite of the curious public.

He murdered 15 young men in London over a five year period and kept the victims' bodies for a certain amount of time after he had killed. Then he dissected them and either burned the remains or flushed them down the toilet.

Viewing the body

In his life he worked as a military chef, police officer and civil servant. Not the usual career progression to serial killer. To stand in such esteemed positions in work and life and then go on to kill is one that has produced conflicting reports from psychologists and experts alike.

His early life consisted of his parents divorcing because of his father becoming an alcoholic. Nilsen was only four-years-old when it happened and his mother remarried soon afterwards. The disruption in the British Isles after the dust of World War Two had settled was felt throughout the nation, more so on the children born into that era.

The fallout of World War Two across many countries is considered one of the reasons for the rise of the serial killer in the Seventies and Eighties. For Nilsen, the break-up of his family at a time of national hardship was crippling.

In his trial and subsequent interviews, Nilsen claimed there was an event in his life, at the age of six-years-old, that was to shape him for many years to come. After his mother remarried, she sent him to live with his grandparents.

It was there that he found a kinship with his grandfather, Andrew Whyte, but after a couple of years he was returned to his mother in 1951. In the Autumn of that year, Nilsen's grandfather died of a heart attack.

Some serial killers have attributed the death of a grandparent as a turning point in their lives. Alexander Pichushkin, the Russian Chessboard Killer, confirmed that after the death of his grandfather he turned to vodka, and then to murder.

What didn't help Nilsen's fragile tendencies at the time was that his mother made him view the body of his grandfather due to her strong religious beliefs. Some psychologists have suggested this was one of the markers that put Nilsen onto a different path.

He later stated that the first time he knew of his grandfather's death was when he saw the corpse. *"It caused a sort of emotional death inside me."* – Dennis Nilsen

Relationship with death

Two years later, when he was eight-years-old, Nilsen almost drowned in the seas close to his hometown. An older boy who was on the coast at the time saw what was happening and went in to rescue him. Nilsen later claimed that the boy masturbated over his body. He awoke from his experience with near death to find ejaculate on his stomach.

Afterwards, he withdrew into himself, hiding away from the world. He was a loner and kept himself to himself but he was never disliked and had many friends at the time. Yet, he preferred to be with his own company.

He had never killed small animals or exhibited a cruel streak towards living things. He was never aggressive or violent towards his peers. He was for all intents and purposes, a good and well-loved child, and the opposite of what a potential serial killer was supposed to have been.

On one occasion he helped in the search of a local man who had gone missing. As fate would have it, it was a young Nilsen and a friend who found the man's body on a riverbank. He later said it had reminded him of seeing the body of his grandfather and upon coming across the corpse he had felt no emotion towards it.

He never had a sexual encounter, nor suffered abuse during his childhood or teenage years. It would be almost two decades later when Nilsen would record his first kill.

The house that death built

He joined the British Army at 17-years-old and stayed there for 11 years. During his military years he said he carried with him a huge weight of loneliness. When he was allowed a private room he would lay down in front of a mirror so he couldn't see his own head in the reflection. He would then masturbate to the sight of what he felt was an unconscious body.

This might in some part have been carried over from his experience on the beach. In 1972 he left the military of his own accord and returned to civilian life. He went on to join the Metropolitan Police in London but only served eight months as an officer before once again leaving of his own accord.

He often witnessed autopsied bodies in close proximity. It fascinated him and he revelled in that part of the job but he left because he felt the job didn't fit him well, having come from the military. In 1974 he went on to work as a civil servant in a job centre in London and became active in trade unions. Then the fantasies he'd long held started to seep into his reality.

There are infamous addresses where killers and murderers have carried out their crimes and lived but none more so than 195 Melrose Avenue. The address in the London area of Cricklewood, would claim 12 victims. He had access to a large garden and was able to burn many of the remains in bonfires. Some of the entrails were thrown over the fence so that local wildlife would consume them.

Nilsen moved into 195 Melrose Avenue, sometimes listed mistakenly as Melrose Place, with a man named David Gallichan. It was said to have been purely a platonic relationship. Nilsen wanted more however, he wanted real commitment and after a series of casual sexual encounters, his bizarre corpse fantasies started to become more prominent.

When he positioned himself in front of a mirror so that his head appeared as missing, he would start to add fake blood to his corpse to look as though he had been killed. He fantasised someone would take him away and bury him and he started to believe that his corpse was the perfect state of his human body.

There was nothing more emotionally and physically pleasing to him than fantasising about his own dead body. After a rough and stressful relationship with Gallichan, Nilsen forced him to leave but was aware of the consequences of being alone. "*Loneliness,*" he wrote, "*is a long unbearable pain.*"

Limpness of the corpse

A day before New Year's Eve, in 1978, Nilsen took his first victim. 14-year-old Stephen Holmes had been refused alcohol at a local pub. Nilsen took the opportunity to invite him to his flat on Melrose Avenue to drink alcohol with him. *"He was to stay with me over the New Year period whether he wanted to or not."*

After going to bed together, Nilsen woke at dawn and became aroused at the sight of his new friend's sleeping body. Holmes was sleeping on his front when Nilsen straddled him and slipped a tie under his neck. He subsequently drowned the young boy in a bucket of water by resting his head over the edge of a chair.

After the bubbles stopped rising from the water, Nilsen rested him on the floor realising that he had just killed a man whose name he did not know. He was also suddenly fearful of the consequences of his actions. Again, a trait not carried by most serial killers.

Nilsen said later that he just sat there staring at the boy's fresh corpse, shaking with the fear and stress of the situation. He made himself a coffee and smoked some cigarettes to ease his nerves.

After washing the corpse in the bathroom he returned Holmes to the bed and was fascinated by the limpness of the corpse. *"It was the beginning of the end of my life as I had known it, I had started down the avenue of death and possession of a new kind of flat-mate."*

Keeping corpses

The concept of keeping corpses as flat-mates was now embedded into Nilsen's psyche. He thought the sight of the corpse was beautiful and not appalling in anyway whatsoever. He hid the body under the floorboards, but after a week had gone by, curiosity had got the better of him – he wanted to see whether the body had changed in anyway.

As he was carrying the body back to the living room, he felt himself becoming aroused and subsequently masturbated onto the corpse's stomach. He even trussed him up by the ankles for an undisclosed amount of time before putting the corpse back under the floorboards.

It would be almost eight months later when Nilsen removed the body to burn it in a bonfire in his garden. He burned rubber to hide the smell and raked the ashes into his garden. Most of his victims were homeless or homosexual men who he would lure to his home with offers of food, alcohol or a place to rest their heads.

His victims were normally killed by strangulation or drowning during the course of the night. He then proceeded to use his butchering skills, learned in the British Army, to help him get rid of the bodies.

He would keep them in various different locations around his home but usually under the floorboards and would constantly engage in sexual activity with the corpses. Over the next three years, Nilsen would murder another 11 men in the ground floor apartment at Melrose Avenue. Of these 11, only four were ever identified.

Kenneth Ockendon was a Canadian tourist he had met at a local pub for lunch in 1979. Nilsen claimed he enjoyed the company of Ockendon and it was the thought of him leaving that drove him to kill again. He strangled him with a headphone cord before washing the body and taking it to bed with him.

Nilsen said he never had sexual intercourse with the corpses but that he did carry out sexual acts with them. He enjoyed masturbating on the corpses and pleasuring himself on certain parts of their bodies. He placed Ockendon under the floorboards and would take the corpse out several times to watch the television with him.

Bodies down the toilet

Nilsen said he would sometimes go into a killing trance and didn't always remember the act of murder. The feeling of control over the corpses of his flat-mates thrilled him and he held a certain fascination with how their corpses deteriorated over time. He believed he was appreciating them more dead than alive.

When the investigation started after Nilsen's arrest, police investigators found over 1000 bone fragments in the garden of 195 Melrose Avenue. He had used the small garden as his own personal burial ground.

Through his butchering career in the British Army he learned the art of butchery so well he would use this skill to rid the house piece by piece of the corpses that remained. He would strip to his underwear and cut them up on the stone floor of his kitchen. He would then place the organs in a plastic bag.

His fantasy progressed to removing the head and then heating it in a large pan of water to boil off the flesh of the skull. He would burn the rest of the remains over time, sometimes close to the garden fence. He was constantly amazed that he was never caught or that no one ever questioned him and his strange activities.

Nilsen one day decided to leave Melrose Avenue and move into a new place in the city. In some part to leave the murderous part of his life behind and in others to escape from the torment he had inflicted. Before Fred and Rose West's 25 Cromwell Street was known to the public, 195

Melrose Avenue was the darkest house of horrors in the British Isles.

In 1981, Nilsen moved to 23 Cranley Gardens and it proved to be his undoing. He found it difficult to get rid of the bodies in his new home and ended up with black bin-liners full of human organs in his wardrobe. He would kill three more at Cranley Gardens over the coming year and a half.

The last victim was dissected in the same way as the previous ones. The head was boiled and the limbs and organs were placed into bags, ready for disposal. But without access to a garden, Nilsen had to come up with different methods of disposal.

He would boil the flesh off the bones and start flushing pieces of the bodies down the toilet.

Rotting flesh

One of the other five tenants who lived in the block complained to the landlord the toilet was not flushing properly. Nilsen had apparently tried to clear the blockage with acid and it mostly worked but it didn't clear the blockage in the external drain.

A local plumber called in a specialist team to get a second opinion and 48 hours later they arrived. One of the technicians, Michael Cattran, went into the drains beneath the house. He found a gooey sludge blocking a part of the sewer coming from a pipe linked to the house.

It appeared to be various pieces of animal flesh and so he immediately reported it to his superiors. When the sewer team left, Nilsen went down into the sewers and started removing the lumps of flesh that had congealed together. But some of the other tenants noticed his movements and strange actions and reported it to the police.

At the same time, the results came back from the analysis of what was assumed to be animal remains. The results were unquestionable; it was human remains. Detectives paid a visit to the house the following evening.

End of a disturbing reign

DCI Peter Jay waited at the scene with two officers for Nilsen to return from work, they followed him into the block of flats and they immediately smelled rotting flesh. Nilsen asked why the police were interested in the drains. They told him they had found human remains.

"Good grief, how awful," Nilsen said.

"Don't mess about, son, where's the rest of the body?" DCI Jay responded.

Nilsen remained relaxed and calmly said that the remains of the bodies were in two plastic bags in the wardrobe. When they drove him to the police station, they asked him how many bodies he was actually talking about.

"Fifteen or sixteen since 1978."

He pleaded guilty with diminished responsibility but on November 4th, 1983, he was sentenced to life imprisonment. He was convicted of six murders and two attempted murders. The Home Secretary later imposed a whole life tariff, which meant that he would never be released and would subsequently be denied any requests for parole.

Nilsen died of natural causes in 2018. His disturbing crimes have been made into various movies, TV series, multiple books, and thousands of articles, each trying to uncover the madness behind the eyes of one of Britain's worst serial killers.

The Mary Russell Murders

In 1828, the Mary Russell brig floated into Cork Harbour, with seven of its crew dead. They had been brutally murdered by their Captain, and the survivors had a disturbing story to tell.

O n the bright morning of 26th June 1828, on what seemed like a perfectly normal day in Cork, Ireland, two ships came into Harbour. The schooner Mary Stubbs and the brig Mary Russell approached the harbour and both had a story to tell.

Some of the people on the dock that morning knew at least part of the story but many were about to discover the horrors that had befallen the Mary Russell. The Mary Stubbs wasn't simply arriving at the harbour as part of its schedule, it was bringing the Mary Russell in, steered by some of their crew.

As the ships came into view, one of the spectators pointed and shouted. Someone had just jumped into the ocean from the Mary Stubbs and they were calling out for him to get rescued. They watched the man swim to nearby ships, before being rescued by one of the smaller ones.

The man they had rescued was Captain William Stewart who was in fear of his life. Unsure if he had been saved or not, Captain Stewart jumped off the rescue boat and back into the water. He was saved yet again by a different boat headed to West Cork.

When the Mary Stubbs and the Mary Russell manage to dock in the late evening, and Captain Stewart was brought ashore, the story of what happened began to unfold. It appeared that two days earlier, on board the Mary Russell, Captain Stewart had murdered seven of his crew.

Madness and mutiny

First mate William Smith, crewmember John Howes, cabin boy Daniel Scully, and an 11-year-old passenger named Thomas Hammond were the only survivors and told their story at the trial of Captain Stewart.

Stewart was considered a good master and kind Captain and had been with the Mary Russell for some time. The ship had left Cork earlier in the year, transporting a cargo of mules to the West Indies in the Caribbean. It picked up a cargo of hides and sugar from Barbados, and departed on 9th May, carrying a crew of six men.

After a week at sea, Stewart wasn't faring well and had been having strange dreams of his men killing him. He began to withdraw from the crew, looking ill and tired, brought on by a lack of sleep. He spoke of his dream to first mate Smith, who attempted to convince him that dreams did not always come true, such was the belief of the time.

One of the crew was James Raynes, an Irishman who had been fired as first mate on another ship due to his alcoholism. Stewart had allowed him to crew for the Mary Russell, somewhat against his better judgement.

Another night came and another dream, this time that God himself was warning Stewart that it would be Raynes who would lead the mutiny and kill him while he slept. This combined with his concerns over Raynes' character, led him to believe that Raynes was going to turn pirate and commandeer his vessel for himself.

Raynes spoke in an Irish dialect that Stewart found hard to understand and it was with this dialect that Raynes conversed and joked with the other crew members – angering the Captain further. Stewart claimed to have overheard the crew asking Raynes to teach them how to navigate and use the stars to help, something only a Captain would have known.

As the weeks passed, Stewart's paranoia grew to such a level that he ordered Smith and his trusted crewmember John Howes, to sleep with him in his cabin for protection, beside numerous weapons.

He accused Raynes of conspiring to mutiny, which was denied vehemently, but Stewart believed in his own mind that mutiny was imminent. He threw navigation equipment and the Captain's log overboard, along with personal belongings.

Six days from Cork Harbour, Stewart took matters into his own hands.

It begins

First mate Smith was out on deck fixing a faulty lamp when Stewart spotted him and believed it to be something untoward. The following morning, he accused him of joining the mutineers and ordered he be tied up against the mast to be lashed for his sins.

The crew voiced their concerns over the legality of the lashing but Smith told them to agree to the Captain's demands. Instead, they tied him up and confined him to a small cellar under the cabin. Seeing what the men had done, he boarded a passing ship to buy meat but returned with a pair of pistols.

Each man was summoned to the Captain's quarters and accused of mutiny, they were tied up as Smith had been, under the threat of being shot in the head if they refused. His trusted crewmember, John Howes, refused to follow Stewart's orders and became involved in a fight with him.

Bloodied and disorientated, Howes succumbed to Stewart's strength and he was tied up with the rest of the crew. Stewart then made cabin boy Scully sign a statement that the crew planned to mutiny. The crew were forced onto the deck overnight where they suffered from the cold and discomfort of the Atlantic waves and weather.

Later on, with the boys' help, they dragged the crew into the cabin, realising their bonds were not good enough to hold them. At that point, Howes broke free, but with the help of the cabin boys, Stewart hit him with an axe and shot him three times. The cabin boy and passenger were promised great riches, which is how Stewart managed to convince them to help him tie his men.

Howes stumbled into the hold, bleeding from three bullet holes. He took refuge behind some crates and would miraculously go onto survive. Stewart didn't search for him but at the back of his mind, he thought Howes may still be alive and could murder him at any moment.

He fixed metal bolts to the cabin floor and tied a rope through each bolt and around the men's necks. It was tied in such a way that when each man moved their head, it would pull on their throats.

With his men tied up below deck, Stewart tried to recall his dreams. He believed that if the crew were innocent of mutinous ideas then God would have sent another ship to rescue them. Believing death to be the only punishment befitting mutiny, he realised what needed to be done.

Slaughter

The Mary Russell dropped its flag to a reversed ensign at half-mast, which was the recognised international distress signal. The previous day, Stewart believed he had seen a ship come close on two occasions but then veer away at the last moment. He believed this to be a sign, and the final nail in the coffin for his crew.

On 22nd June, Stewart stormed into the cabin area with a crowbar and screamed at the top of his voice, "*the curse of God is on you all, there's the ship come to us twice and went away. You ruffians, you ruffians, you were going to take my life, but I'll take yours.*"

Stewart beat the second mate over the head repeatedly until his skull had been crushed.

Seeing this as the only way to kill mutinous crew members, he moved between each of the mean beating, cutting, and smashing them to death.

After Stewart had brutally murdered seven of his crew, he turned to the boys and showed them his steady hand. "*Look, boys, at my hand, how steady it is. I think no more of killing them than if they were dogs.*"

Stewart then stood outside of the cellar where first mate Smith was restrained, put a harpoon to the air-hole that had been cut for him, and fired the weapon. The harpoon hit Smith in the eye, shoulder, ear and face, but he went on to survive. Stewart thought him to be dead as the point of the harpoon had hit the hides in storage, which had sounded like human flesh.

Later, when the Mary Russell had come ashore, a witness to the scene on the ship, had the following to say.

"*There were seven human beings with their skulls so battered, that scarcely a vestige of them was left for recognition, with a frightful mess of coagulated blood, all strewed about the cabin. Nearly a hundredweight of cords binding down their bodies to strong iron bolts, which had been driven into the floor for that murderous purpose. Some of the bodies were bound round about six places, and with several coils of rope round their necks, and all were in a state of decomposition, so that it required a constitution of no ordinary strength to bear up against the spectacle, and the effluvia that arose from a confined cabin.*"

The Mary Stubbs

Captain Robert Callendar of the American schooner Mary Stubbs was on the way back from Barbados to Belfast, carrying various cargos, when he noticed the Mary Russell flying the distress signal. They were 300 miles from the Cove of Cork when they approached the ship.

Callendar was an American from New Brunswick and no stranger to the Atlantic trade routes. He ordered the Mary Stubbs to approach the Russell with caution, due to pirates that had recently been seen in the area.

After calling out for some time, Captain Stewart finally appeared from the cabin, covered in blood. Stewart immediately told Callendar that he had executed nine men for mutiny, believing Smith and Howes to be dead, and bragged it about to Callendar.

He led Callendar to the cabin where the seven crew members had been slaughtered and claimed that he was truly a valiant man to have killed so many so easily. Suddenly, Smith and Howes climbed out of the hold and begged for Callendar's help.

Captain Callendar took the two men to his own ship and then ordered three of his own crew to get on board the Russell and follow the Stubbs into Cork. Immediately, believing the three new crew members to be enemies and assassins, Stewart jumped overboard and began swimming away. But Callendar had him fished out of the water and placed in the hold of the Mary Stubbs.

Stewart was put on trial on 11th August 1828 and pleaded not guilty on the grounds that he was insane and incapable of knowing right from wrong. Press at the time reported Stewart as being in a state of mental derangement.

When Dr Thomas Carey Osborne of the Cork Asylum took the stand to explain the insanity, he diagnosed Captain Stewart with monomania. It was a 19th-century psychiatric term that meant a form of partial insanity conceived as a single pathological preoccupation in an otherwise sound mind. Meaning that someone would run with an insane notion while being quite sane at the same time. We would now refer to this as psychosis.

Captain Stewart was found not guilty of murder due to being under mental derangement. He was committed to the Cork Asylum for Criminal Lunatics. A number of years later, Stewart had another psychotic episode and murdered a hospital attendant with a weapon made from animal bones. He was never released, spent time in various asylums, and died of natural causes in 1873.

So that people would never forget the victims of the Mary Russell, a family member pooled funds together and had a gravestone inscribed, which still stands at Cill Muire cemetery. It reads:

'You, gentle reader that pass this way, Attend awhile, adhere to what I say.

By murder vile I was bereft of life and parted from two lovely babes and wife.

By Captain Stewart I met an early doom on board the Mary Russell the 22nd of June.

Forced from this world, to meet my God on high, with whom I hope to reign eternally nigh.'

The Reality TV Swindler

How a down-on-his-luck homeless man conned fame-seeking wannabes to take part in a year-long reality TV show that didn't exist.

The Great Reality TV Swindle, AKA: Project MS-2, was a con devised and enacted by a British man calling himself Nik Russian. He had placed advertisements in national publications seeking people to audition for a new year-long reality television show for Channel 4 in the UK.

After receiving hundreds of applications from eager fame-seeking reality TV fans, he held auditions at a location called Raven's Ait, which is a small island on the Thames between Surbiton and Kingston, usually used for conferences and weddings.

There, he whittled down the applicants to 30 successful people who would take part. Without telling them that the show hadn't actually been commissioned. He gave them bizarre instructions that many decided didn't add up and left the show before it started.

Russian instructed them to leave their homes, quit their jobs, and meet in London on a specific date in the early Summer of 2002. They signed contracts that meant nothing and left their lives behind for the chance to be on the show.

The Man

Nik Russian was no TV producer, even though he acted like one around the contestants, and managed to charm them into believing a TV show was on the cards. Unfortunately for the contestants on the show, the programme didn't really exist.

He claimed the show was a secret and it went under the name of Project MS-2, to put off curious parties. At the auditions, he had enlisted the help of his friends to be the cameraman, a psychological analyst, and showrunners, all unaware the programme was fake.

Nik Russian wasn't quite who he said he was. Born Keith Anthony Gillard in Surrey in 1977, he went through a series of name changes and personas including Jack Lister and the Nikita Russian. He studied English at the University of London, wrote a series of unpublished books, and set up multiple businesses that failed.

By the time he came up with the idea for the show he was working as a customer assistant at the bookstore, Waterstones. When the show went into 'production' on 10th June 2002, Nik left his job, ended the tenancy on his flat, and became literally homeless.

On the 10th of June, the 30 contestants were split into three teams of 10 and instructed to meet at different locations across London. It was only then they discovered what the challenge was.

The Plan

The challenge for the show was to make £1million (GBP) in one year by any means possible as a team. The prize? – £100,000 each. Confused by the point of making their own prize money, many of the wannabe TV stars rebelled.

Despite having signed sketchy contracts, the entirety of Team One and Team Three left the show and returned to lives they had temporarily ended. For many, this meant they had to move back in with the parents, having ended relationships and jobs – such was the allure of reality TV fame.

Team Two had no idea the other teams had left the show and were handed their first challenge by the cameraman. The cameraman was Tim Eagle, an eager trainee who had taken on the job for free to gain experience in the industry.

The first task was to find accommodation for free for one week. They also had to find food for free as the production wasn't going to feed them. On that first day in London, many of Team Two were confused by the fact they would be making money themselves that they would keep, but they saw it is a stepping-stone to that all-important fame.

To help them find free accommodation, Tim suggested they could sleep in his house until they found better dwellings. Team Two ended up sleeping on his floor, in the hope that fame and fortune were just around the corner. But something was off and one part of the challenge didn't seem legit.

To ensure the contestants were making money – towards that £1million target, they had to deposit their funds into a bank account owned by Russian, which Russian claimed was to track how much they were making.

The Collapse

After the first night, Team Two were concerned they were being played, and were worried that

Tim knew nothing about the programme beyond the fact he had to film them. They decided to use Tim's camera to make their own reality show, while questioning Nik Russian's motives at the same time.

It was at that point that Russian stopped taking phone calls from the team. Some of Team Two left that night but others including Louise Miles, Debbie Driver, and Daniel Pope, remained.

That night, unable to maintain the scam any longer, Russian arrived at Tim's house – as he was homeless – and suggested it was a good idea if he stayed with Team Two. Russian confessed there was no programme commission and the contracts were fake.

On the 12th of June, two days since production had started, Tim contacted the London Tonight news team and said he had a story for them. Aware they had been scammed, the remaining members of Team Two locked Russian in Tim's flat and waited for journalists to arrive.

After answering a few questions, Russian went into hiding and for a while was nowhere to be seen, but a real TV show was on his case. The day after Russian vanished, Debbie contacted two executives, Caz Gorham and Frances Dickenson of indie production company Christmas Television.

When they were told all the details of the swindle, the company decided to produce a special one-off documentary film about what had happened. But of course, they first had to convince the contestants that they were to make a real programme about them, and not a con job.

The Commission

Amazingly, Channel 4, who Russian lied had commissioned the reality TV series, ended up commissioning the documentary from Christmas Television. One of the contestants wasn't sure the documentary was real until a production team turned up with a 'real camera'.

The aim of the documentary was to expose the swindle and show how the participants were trying to get their lives back together. Realising that Tim the cameraman and other 'production' crew had provided everything for free and were not getting paid, Christmas Television included them in their documentary.

Louise uncovered the truth that Russian's production company didn't even exist, and that the person who took their phone calls in the early days was Russian's mother, Margaret. Daniel tracked down Russian to an address in Richmond and convinced him to be interviewed for the documentary.

The most curious aspect of the story was that Russian believed he had not done anything wrong. He hadn't taken any money from the contestants, nor had he committed a crime, though there were signs that down the line once money started coming in that a crime may have been committed.

He genuinely believed – in the age of reality TV – that his idea for a show would work and that once he presented the series to a production company that it would be purchased and run on TV. But he never got that far, and for many of the contestants, they returned to broken lives, at the tail-end of a confused dream that one man had.

Silver lining

Many had thrown huge going away parties, given away possessions, ended tenancies or sold homes, and some even ended relationships, all for the chance of reality TV success. The official documentary team spent months tracking Russian down, as he moved around a lot within London.

For many of the contestants, though initially feeling sorry for him and his lost dream, pity turned to anger. Many saw him for the conman he was, and that he had psychologically abused many people in order to trick them into earning money for him.

Though he put his own life on the line to make the project work, it remained unforgiveable that he ended up hurting so many people. Many contestants fell into depression and needed a lot of support to get them back into the world.

The documentary was called The Great Reality TV Swindle and was shown on Channel 4 in December 2002. Much of the reaction to the documentary was split. Many placed the blame wholly on Russian for being an unscrupulous conman but some claimed him to be a tragic figure of overstretched ambition.

Some critics – before the heady days of social media – placed the blame squarely on the contestants and the nature of reality TV itself, with The Scotsman newspaper calling them 'gullible wannabes'.

There was an ironic twist for the contestants, that despite the con, it led them to actually appear on TV, not as the wide-eyed eager wannabes in the homemade videos, but as reflective, wounded individuals.

It remains unclear what happened to Russian but with his charming, good looks, and desire to hit the big time, it wouldn't be a surprise if he popped up somewhere else, in another time, with a new name – and a new con.

Murder at Beachy Head

A young woman disappeared near Beachy Head, a known suicide spot, but nine years later, her body is discovered on top of the cliffs, with links to an infamous serial killer.

Eastbourne, on the South Coast of England, is a Victorian coastal town popular with tourists for its beaches and history. Its long promenade offers a pier, Victorian hotels, shops, and a shingle beach with sandy stretches at low tide.

Immediately to the west of the town is Beachy Head, the highest chalk sea cliffs in Great Britain, and part of the South Downs National Park, which stretches 87 miles along the coast to the ancient city of Winchester.

Though beautiful and alluring, attracting artists and writers from all over the world, Beachy Head harbours a darkness. Since the 7th Century, it has been Britain's most common suicide spot, and the third most common suicide spot in the world, after San Francisco's Golden Gate Bridge, and Japan's Aokigahara Woods.

On Wednesday 15th May 1980, 22-year-old Eastbourne College student Jessie Earl, disappeared from her bedsit and failed to return home the next morning. The London born student was known to take long walks up to Beachy Head where she would read and write about nature.

So when she disappeared, and a police search turned up no trace of her, it was suggested she had become part of the saddening statistics that had haunted Beachy Head for centuries. Until her remains were discovered on the cliff top nine years later.

1980

On the night of the 15th, Jessie had phoned her mother from a phone box on the seafront and told her that she would be home to London for a visit on the Friday. But on Saturday the 18th, when Jessie had failed to show up, and concerned for her whereabouts, her mother, Valerie, caught the train down to Eastbourne.

She arrived at Jessie's bedsit in Upperton Gardens and found her purse and personal belongings on the bed. Dirty dishes in the sink suggested she left them to soak before returning to clean them later, but she never returned, and her friends claimed they hadn't seen her since the Wednesday.

Jessie was officially reported missing and the police used sniffer dogs to search the bedsit for clues. Missing person posters were put up around town, and the media were informed that Jessie had failed to return home.

Police used helicopters and thermal imaging to search the South Downs on Beachy Head, expecting the worst, but there were no signs of Jessie anywhere. After three weeks, the investigation ground to a halt and it was left to the family to continue appealing for new information.

Valerie found Jessie's diary in the bedsit and it contained no suggestion she was suffering from ill mental health or considering suicide. For nine years, Valerie, and her husband, John, refused to believe the suicide version of events.

1989

On a fresh March day in 1989, a family were flying kites on top of Beachy Head when one of the kites fell into a dense section of shrub land. When the father went to retrieve the kite, he discovered the skeletal remains of a human body.

A forensic investigation confirmed they were the remains of Jessie Earl. They discovered she had died at the scene and was found naked. The only item of clothing was a bra tied around her wrists, and all personal items such as her ring and watch were missing.

The investigation was so detailed that police cordoned off an area of land where she had been found and excavated the soil to search for clues that would have been left nine years earlier. They found nothing in the soil, and a local team of metal detectors came up short too.

Despite being found naked and with a bra tied around her wrists, the coroner later recorded an open verdict, as he could find no evidence to conclusively prove how she had died.

John Earl confirmed the family's stance that she had been murdered. *'Jesse didn't get herself killed by accident, suicide, or anything else. She was naked, she had been tied up with her bra. She was murdered.'*

Operation Anagram

Eleven years passed, and in 2000, the police launched a murder enquiry into the death of Jessie Earl, brought about by the appeals made by her family. However, the lead investigator admitted they had destroyed vital evidence.

Because Jessie's death was never officially classified as a murder, the forensic evidence had been destroyed in 1997, in line with police procedures. This included the bra, and some of the soil that had been removed from around the body. Due to the lack of forensic evidence, the case went nowhere.

Then in 2006, a convicted rapist, who had spent 14 years in prison for the assault and rape of two teenage girls in Leigh Park, Havant, was arrested for the murder of Angelika Kluk in Glasgow. His name was Peter Tobin, and he would soon become known as one of Britain's worst serial killers.

After his conviction in the same year for the murder of Angelika, a nationwide police investigation was set up to look at Tobin's life and movements before his first prison sentence, and in the years between being released and the 2006 victim.

They called this investigation; Operation Anagram, and it used multiple police forces and databases to link Tobin to dozens of murders and disappearances of teenage girls and young women across the United Kingdom. One of them was Jessie Earl.

One case he was positively linked to was 18-year-old Louise Kay who disappeared from none other than Beachy Head in 1988. Tobin was known to have been working at an Eastbourne hotel at the time and may have lured Louise to his home in Brighton, a few miles along the coast to the east.

Louise's body has never been found but is suspected to have buried by Tobin at one of his properties.

A likely theory

In 2007, while searching one of Tobin's old houses in Bathgate, Scotland, they unearthed the bodies of 15-year-old Vicky Hamilton and Dinah McNicol, who had both disappeared in 1991. Vicky was found with her wrists tied together with a bra.

The similarities to the discovery of Jessie's remains were overwhelming but not conclusive. Operation Anagram investigators pored over Jessie's cases and confirmed Tobin was living in the area at the time. But without the evidence destroyed by the police, and no confession from Tobin, they could not charge him with the murder.

Operation Anagram went quiet in 2011 with no more victims to look at, and no new information coming to light. Since his arrest in 2006, Tobin has been convicted of three murders at different trials, with a suggestion he may have killed up to 10. He was sentenced to life imprisonment.

Jessie's family believe that Tobin may have been responsible for her death. But Tobin presents a problem. Many unsolved murders and disappearances from the 1970s and 1980s, tend to be at some point linked to Tobin and another British serial killer, Robert Black.

As Tobin and Black were active during that time period, and moved about a lot, it seems easy to match them up with various unsolved cases. But the problem comes when too many victims are laid at their feet, as it may hinder investigations looking elsewhere at other suspects or circumstances that could hold more truth.

In 2018, it was confirmed by local police that there was no hard evidence implicating Tobin or any other suspect in the murder of Jessie Earl. Despite the murder enquiries into Jessie's death, the official death certificate remains an open verdict, something her family are fighting to change.

It is possible and likely that Jessie was killed by Peter Tobin. It's also possible she was murdered by another unidentified killer, someone who has never been suspected. For over forty years, her murder has remained unsolved.

The only witness is Beachy Head itself, which continues to harbour the secrets of the dead, among hundreds of thousands of the living who visit for its beauty.

The Cracks Terror

In old London, women were arming themselves and men were crossdressing to catch a mysterious buttock beater, who would lift women's skirts and spank them before retreating to the dark alleyways.

I n the year of our Lord, 1681, a curious fellow was patrolling the shadows of London's Strand, Fleet Street, and Holborn. He would hide in dimly lit alleyways, waiting for his prey to come close.

When lone women were near, the attacker would jump out of the shadows, lift their skirts and slap their behinds with his bare hands or a rod. Occasionally the attacks were accompanied with a guttural cry of '*Spanko*'.

The attacker would then escape into the alleyways of 17th Century London, leaving his victims shivering in fear and humiliation. His crimes were considered so serious that male friends of the victims came up with an unusual method to try and catch him.

Attacks from the bottom beater were increasing rapidly and the police were already losing control of the situation. In fact, the 1681 buttock beater was the second of three waves of spanking attacks in the British Capital.

The third, in 1712, garnered the name of Whipping Tom, which is used to refer to all three attackers.

Lurking

The first wave, the original Whipping Tom, began nine years earlier in 1672 but not much information is known about that version of the spanker. Aside from a one-sentence newspaper clipping that suggested he was an '*enemy to the milk-wenches bums*'.

The first known attack of the 1681 Whipping Tom was upon a servant maid near Fleet Street. The maid had been sent out to look for her master and was walking near a dimly lit alley when she saw a man drinking near the wall, with his back to her.

The moment she passed him, the man violently grabbed her, threw her to the ground, dragged her up over his knee and spanked her until she screamed for help. Then in a flash, the attacker pushed her into a wall and vanished down the maze of alleyways in the city.

From then, the attacks were almost daily, forcing women to carry penknives and scissors in case they too were bent over the knee and attacked. There was an outcry towards police who were deemed ineffective and unable to catch the attacker, which led to...

Vigilante crossdressers

The Metropolitan Police Service would not be created for another 200 years, and the organisation of law enforcement in the 17th Century was lacking. People could not trust their government to help them and so the vigilante's took over.

To catch the attacker, male friends of the victims dressed up as women and lurked around the alleyways. They hoped they would be a target for the mysterious spanker. Not for their own pleasure, mind you, but for the pleasure of catching the buttock beater.

Though there are no reports as to how many men dressed as women to catch Whipping Tom, there were stories of the time about groups of crossdressers secretly parading the locations where the attacks had taken place.

The vigilante groups eventually led to the arrest of a local haberdasher and an accomplice. They were put on trial for the attacks but due to records being misplaced over the centuries, there is no information to the punishment they received, or their names.

So how did the name of Whipping Tom come about?

1712

31 years later, in the London Borough of Hackney, the attacks began again. The previous two attackers had been forgotten when the third Whipping Tom began stalking lone women in the alleyways of the city.

Except this time, Whipping Tom had a motive. A man named Thomas Wallis was suffering from a broken heart. He had fallen in love with a beautiful woman who it appeared had played with his heart, or in his own words from his later confession, she had been '*barbarously false*' to him.

Perhaps 'barbarously false' was old London speak for adulterous behaviour, or perhaps she had turned down his advances in favour of another. Regardless, Thomas vowed to seek his revenge, not only against the one he so dearly loved – but all women.

On 10th October 1712, Thomas claimed his first victim. He pulled some strong branches off a birch tree and headed off into the night to find his victim. He didn't have to wait long. As he was walking through a field, he noticed a woman wandering alone.

He approached her from behind, lifted up her skirt, and beat her on the buttocks with his branches. Then, like the Whipping Tom's before him, he vanished into the night, as quick as he had come.

The Cracks Terror

In his later confession, Thomas claimed he wanted to beat at least 100 women before Christmas of 1712. To achieve his goal, he would go out each night, and on occasion attack multiple women. He was known to have kept a written account of the beatings.

By 1st December, he had hit a target of beating the buttocks of 70 women, giving him the unruly newspaper moniker of 'The Cracks Terror'. He was captured due to an increased police presence in the city.

Thomas was handed down a sentence of one year in prison. There are stories online claiming he was subjected to spankings from women twice weekly, but there are no official records to back this up. Though it would have been a fitting punishment.

Over the years, the name of Whipping Tom has been used to link the three buttock beaters of London, where the names of the first two buttock beaters have gone unrecorded. For some women, from the cries of *'Spanko'*, to the beatings of the birch, Whipping Tom made an ineradicable mark on their lives.

There have been many serial spankers over the years, with one as recent as 2017, in Spokane, Washington. 28-year-old Jonathan Smith slapped the backsides of dozens of women along the popular Centennial hiking trail, before fleeing like the Whipping Tom of old. He was caught when he made a tearful confession to a local TV station.

Despite the legacy the Whipping Toms have left on bizarre true crime, it appears they were the first known buttock beaters in modern history. So much so, that poems and ditties were written about them – to warn women walking alone at night.

And now the Female Clubs go down,
Which frequent were about that Town;
For fear that Whipping-Tom should meet
Them as they ramble in the Street;
And each does seek to save her Bum,
From the fierce rage of Whipping-Tom:
Then females 'ware how late you stray,
Lest Whipping-Tom your Buttocks pay.

Look for more in the Orrible British True Crime Series!

OUT NOW!

For bibliographies, citations, true crime blog posts, more true crime books, and more information on new releases for your collection, head on over to www.benoakley.co.uk

Printed in Great Britain
by Amazon

45594005R00089